W9-BIH-432

SECRET CODES 2003

VOLUME 2

//////BRADYGAMES®
TAKE YOUR GAME FURTHER

Contents

PlayStation® 2

AMPLITUDE

Blur

During a game, press R3 (x4), L3 (x4), R3.

Monkey Notes

During a game, press L3 (x4), R3 (x4), L3. Quit the game and go back into the song to see the effect. Reenter the code to disable it.

Random Note Placement

During a game, press **X**, **X**, Left, Left, R3, R3, Right, Right. Quit the game and go back into the song to see the effect. Reenter the code to disable it.

Change Shape of Track Layout

During the game, press L3 (x3), R3 (x3), L3, R3, L3. Quit the game and go back into the song to see the effect. Enter it once for a tunnel look and a second time for a Tempest-style look. Reenter the code to disable it.

ATV OFFROAD FURY 2

Select Profile Editor, Unlock Items, then Cheats, and enter the following:

Unlock Everything
Enter **IGIVEUP**.

All ATVs
Enter **SHOWROOM**.

All Equipment
Enter **THREADS**.

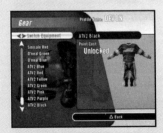

All Tracks
Enter **TRLBLAZR**.

San Jacinto Isles

Enter GABRIEL.

All Games

Enter GAMEON.

All Championship Events

Enter GOLDCUPS.

1,000 Profile Points

Enter GIMMEPTS.

Disable Wrecks

Enter FLYPAPER. Reenter the code to enable wrecks again.

Aggressive AI

Enter EATDIRT. Reenter the code to disable aggressive AI.

ATV QUAD POWER RACING 2

Enter the following as a profile name. You will get a message if entered correctly.

All Riders
Enter BUBBA.

Maximum Stats
Enter GINGHAM.

All ATVs
Enter GENERALLEE.

Champs
Enter REDROOSTER.

All Tracks
Enter ROADKILL.

Challenges
Enter DOUBLEBARREL.

All Tricks
Enter FIDDLERSELBOW.

BATTLE ENGINE AQUILA

Level Select

Start a new game and enter !EVAH! as a name.

God Mode

Start a new game and enter B4K42 as a name. Pause the game to find this option.

All Extras

Start a new game and enter 105770Y2 as a name.

BIG MUTHA TRUCKERS

All Cheats

Enter CHEATINGMUTHATRUCKER as a code.

Evil Truck

Enter VARLEY as a code.

Fast Truck

Enter GINGERBEER as a code.

$10 Million

Enter LOTSAMONEY as a code.

Level Select

Enter LAZYPLAYER as a code.

Unlimited Time

Enter PUBLICTRANSPORT as a code.

Disable Damage

Enter 6WL as a code.

Automatic Sat Nav

Enter USETHEFORCE as a code.

Diplomatic Immunity

Enter VICTORS as a code.

Small Pedestrians

Enter DAISHI as a code.

BLACK AND BRUISED

Intercontinental Mode

Select Cheat Codes from the Setup menu and press
START, **X** (x3), ● (x3), ■ (x3), START.

Second Skin

Select Cheat Codes from the Setup menu and press
START, **X**, R1, ●, ■, START.

All Boxers

Select Cheat Codes from the Setup menu and press
START, **X**, ●, ■, ■, R1, R1, ■, ●, **X**, START.

Scrap Yard Scene

Select Cheat Codes from the Setup menu and press
START, ●, R1, ●, R1, **X**, **X**, START.

Conversation Mode

Select Cheat Codes from the Setup menu and press
START, R1, **X**, ●, ■, R1 (x3), START.

Invulnerability

Select Cheat Codes from the Setup menu and press
START, **X**, **X**, ●, ●, R1, R1, ■, ■, START. Enter with
Controller 2 for Invulnerability for Boxer 2.

All Boxer's Life

Select Cheat Codes from the Setup menu and press
START, **X**, **■**, **●**, R1, **X**, **■**, **●**, R1, START.

Double Speed

Select Cheat Codes from the Setup menu and press
START, R1 (x10), START.

Constant Powerup

Select Cheat Codes from the Setup menu and press
START, **X**, **●**, **X**, **●**, **X**, **●**, **■** (x3), START. Enter with
Controller 2 to get Constant Powerup for Boxer 2.

CONFLICT: DESERT STORM

Cheat Mode

At the Main menu, press **■**, **■**, **●**, **●**, L1, L1, R1, R1, L2, L2,
R2, R2. Pause the game to find the Cheats option.

CONFLICT ZONE

Money

Pause the game and press **X**, Left, Right, Up, Left.

CONTRA: SHATTERED SOLDIER

30 Lives

At the Main menu, press Up, Up, Down, Down, L1, R1, L2, R2, L3, R3 with a second controller.

DEAD TO RIGHTS

From the Main menu, hold L1 + L2 + R1 + R2 and enter the following cheats:

Lazy Mode

Press Down, Left, Down, ▲, Down.

10,000 Bullets Mode

Press Up, Left, Down, Right, ●.

Time To Play

Press ■, ■, ●, ●, Right.

One Shot Kill

Press ▲, ●, ●, ●, Left.

Sharpshooter Mode

Press ■, ■, ■, Down, Right.

Bang-bang Cheat

Press ●, ▲, ■, ●, Right.

Precursor

Press Up, Up, Down, Down, Up.

Super Cop Mode
Press ■, ▲, Left, Up, Right.

Woof!
Press ●, ■, ▲, ●, Down.

Gimme Some Sugar, Baby
Press Left, Right, Left, ●, ■.

Bulletproof Mode
Press Up, Up, Up, ■, Down.

Chow Yun Jack Mode
Press ▲, ●, Up, Up, Up.

Up Close and Personal Mode
Press ■, ▲, ●, ▲, ■.

Extraordinary Skills
Press ●, ●, Up, Up, ■.

Fight Club
Press Right, ■, Left, ●, ▲.

Invisible Jack Mode
Press ▲, ▲, Up, Up, ▲.

Boomstick Mode
Press Right, ●, ●, ●, ■.

Hard Boiled Mode
Press ▲, ■, Left, Left, ●.

Wussy Mode
Press ■, Left, ▲, Up, Down.

DEF JAM VENDETTA

Arii
At the Character select, hold L1 + L2 + R1 + R2 and press X, ■, ▲, ●, ■.

Briggs Alternate Costume
At the Character select, hold L1 + L2 + R1 + R2 and press X, ▲, ●, ■, ●.

Carla
At the Character select, hold L1 + L2 + R1 + R2 and press X, ■, X (x3).

Chukklez

At the Character select, hold L1 + L2 + R1 + R2 and press ■, ■, ▲, X, ●.

Cruz

At the Character select, hold L1 + L2 + R1 + R2 and press ●, ▲, X, X, ●.

D-Mob

At the Character select, hold L1 + L2 + R1 + R2 and press ■, ■, ▲, ■, ■.

Dan G

At the Character select, hold L1 + L2 + R1 + R2 and press X, ●, X, ●, ■.

Deebo

At the Character select, hold L1 + L2 + R1 + R2 and press ●, ●, X, X, ▲.

Deja

At the Character select, hold L1 + L2 + R1 + R2 and press ●, ■, ●, ●, X.

DMX

At the Character select, hold L1 + L2 + R1 + R2 and press ●, X, ●, ▲, ■.

Drake: Alternate Costume

Press X, ▲, ▲, ●, ●.

Funkmaster Flex

At the Character select, hold L1 + L2 + R1 + R2 and press ●, ▲, ●, ●, ■.

Headache

At the Character select, hold L1 + L2 + R1 + R2 and press ▲(x3), ■, ●.

House

At the Character select, hold L1 + L2 + R1 + R2 and press ▲, X, ▲, ●, X.

Iceberg

At the Character select, hold L1 + L2 + R1 + R2 and press ■, ▲, ●, ■, ●.

Ludacris

At the Character select, hold L1 + L2 + R1 + R2 and press ●(x3), ■, ▲.

Manny Alternate Costume

At the Character select, hold L1 + L2 + R1 + R2 and press ●, ■, ●, ■, ●.

Masa

At the Character select, hold L1 + L2 + R1 + R2 and press X, ●, ▲, ■, ■.

Method Man

At the Character select, hold L1 + L2 + R1 + R2 and press ■, ●, X, ▲, ●.

Moses

At the Character select, hold L1 + L2 + R1 + R2 and press ▲, ▲, ■, ■, X.

N.O.R.E.

At the Character select, hold L1 + L2 + R1 + R2 and press ●, ■, ▲, X, ●.

Nyne

At the Character select, hold L1 + L2 + R1 + R2 and press ■, ●, X, X, ▲.

Omar

At the Character select, hold L1 + L2 + R1 + R2 and press ●, ●, ■, ▲, ▲.

Opal

At the Character select, hold L1 + L2 + R1 + R2 and press ●, ●, ■, ■, ▲.

Peewee

At the Character select, hold L1 + L2 + R1 + R2 and press **X**, **X**, ■, ▲, ■.

Peewee Alternate Costume

At the Character select, hold L1 + L2 + R1 + R2 and press **X**, ▲, ▲, ■, ●.

Penny

At the Character select, hold L1 + L2 + R1 + R2 and press **X** (x3), ▲, ●.

Pockets

At the Character select, hold L1 + L2 + R1 + R2 and press ▲, ■, ●, ■, **X**.

Proof Alternate Costume

At the Character select, hold L1 + L2 + R1 + R2 and press **X**, ■, ▲, ■, ●.

Razor

At the Character select, hold L1 + L2 + R1 + R2 and press ▲, ■, ▲, ●, **X**.

Razor Alternate Costume

At the Character select, hold L1 + L2 + R1 + R2 and press ■, ●, **X**, ▲, ▲.

Redman

At the Character select, hold L1 + L2 + R1 + R2 and press ●, ●, ▲, ■, **X**.

Ruffneck

At the Character select, hold L1 + L2 + R1 + R2 and press **X**, ■, **X**, ▲, ●.

Ruffneck Alternate Costume

At the Character select, hold L1 + L2 + R1 + R2 and press ■, ●, ▲, **X**, ■.

Scarface

At the Character select, hold L1 + L2 + R1 + R2 and press ●, ■, X, ▲, ■.

Steel

At the Character select, hold L1 + L2 + R1 + R2 and press X, ▲, ●, ●, ▲.

Sketch

At the Character select, hold L1 + L2 + R1 + R2 and press ▲, ▲, ●, ■, X.

Tank Alternate Costume

At the Character select, hold L1 + L2 + R1 + R2 and press ▲, ■, ●, X, X.

Snowman

At the Character select, hold L1 + L2 + R1 + R2 and press ▲, ▲, X, X, ●.

T'ai

At the Character select, hold L1 + L2 + R1 + R2 and press ●, ●, ■, X, ●.

Spider Alternate Costume

At the Character select, hold L1 + L2 + R1 + R2 and press ■, ▲, X, ■, ●.

Zaheer

At the Character select, hold L1 + L2 + R1 + R2 and press ▲, ▲, ■, X, X.

DEVIL MAY CRY 2

Dante and Lucia Bonus Diesel Costume

Play the first mission and save. Reset the game and at the Press Start screen, press L3, R3, L1, R1, L2, R2, L3, R3.

DR. MUTO

Select Cheats from the Options menu and enter the following:

Invincibility

Enter NECROSCI. This doesn't help you when you fall from high above.

Never Take Damage

Enter CHEATERBOY.

Unlock Every Gadget

Enter TINKERTOY.

Unlock Every Morph

Enter EUREKA.

Go Anywhere

Enter BEAMMEUP.

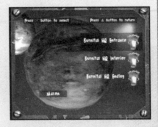

Secret Morphs

Enter LOGGLOGG.

See the Movies

Enter HOTTICKET.

Super Ending

Enter BUZZOFF.

DROME RACERS

Win Race

At the Main menu, press Left, Right, Left, Right, Up, Down, Up, Down, ■, ▲, ●. Press L3 to win.

All Tracks in Arcade Mode

At the Main menu, press Left, Right, Left, Right, Up, Down, Up, Down, ▲, ▲, X.

Six Cars in Two-Player Mode Races

At the Main menu, press Left, Right, Left, Right, Up, Down, Up, Down, ■, ■, X.

Wireframe Mode

At the Main menu, press Left, Right, Left, Right, Up, Down, Up, Down, ●, ●, X.

Purple Rain

At the Main menu, press Left, Right, Left, Right, Up, Down, Up, Down, Up, Down, ● (x3).

Cow

At the Main menu, press Left, Right, Left, Right, Up, Down, Up, Down, Up, Down, Up, Down, ● (x3).

ENTER THE MATRIX

Cheats

After playing through the hacking system and unlocking CHEAT.EXE, you can use CHEAT.EXE to enter the following. WARNING! Turn off the All Guns cheat for the third level, or the game will crash.

Infinite Ammo	1DDF2556
All Guns	0034AFFF
Invisibility	FFFFFFF1
Infinite Focus	69E5D9E4
Infinite Health	7F4DF451
Speedy Logos	7867F443
Unlock Secret Level	13D2C77F

EVOLUTION SKATEBOARDING

All Secret Characters

Press Up, Down, Left, Right, Up, Down, Left, Right, Up, Down, Left, Right, ●.

Level Select

Press L2, R2, Left, Right, Left, Right, Left, Right, Down, Down, Up, Up, Down, Up.

FISHERMAN'S BASS CLUB

Line Doesn't Break

Before you cast, press L1, R1, R1, R2, ▲, ●, R2.

GHOST RECON

All Missions

At the Title screen, press **X**, L2, ▲, R2, Select.

All Special Features

At the Title screen, press L1, L2, R1, R2, **X**, Select.

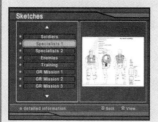

Invincibility

Pause the game and press L1, R2, L2, R1, Select.

GRAND THEFT AUTO: VICE CITY

Enter the following cheats during a game. Some of these cheats may affect your game play. Don't save your progress, unless you are sure you want this effect.

Health Cheat

Press R1, R2, L1, ●, Left, Down, Right, Up, Left, Down, Right, Up.

Armor Cheat

Press R1, R2, L1, **X**, Left, Down, Right, Up, Left, Down, Right, Up.

Low Gravity

Press Right, R2, ●, R1, L2, Down, L1, R1.

Better Driving

Press ▲, R1, R1, Left, R1, L1, R2, L1. Use L3 to make vehicle jump.

Suicide

Press Right, L2, Down, R1, Left, Left, R1, L1, L2, L1.

Wanted Level Up 2

Press R1, R1, ●, R2, Left, Right, Left, Right, Left, Right.

Wanted Level Down 2

Press R1, R1, ●, R2, Up, Down, Up, Down, Up, Down.

Slow Motion

Press ▲, Up, Right, Down, ■, R2, R1.

Faster Time

Press ●, ●, L1, ■, L1, ■, ■, ■, L1, ▲, ●, ▲.

Black Cars

Press ●, L2, Up, R1, Left, **X**, R1, L1, Left, ●.

Pink Cars

Press ●, L1, Down, L2, Left, **X**, R1, L1, Right, ●.

Change Wheels

Press R1, **X**, **▲**, Right, R2, **■**, Up, Down, **■**.

Car Speed x2

Press R1, R2, L1, L1, Left, Down, Right, Up, Left, Down, Right, Up.

Cars Float

Press Right, R2, **●**, R1, L2, **■**, R1, R2.

All Cars Explode

Press R2, L2, R1, L1, L2, R2, **■**, **▲**, **●**, **▲**, L2, L1.

Robocops

Press **●**, L1, Down, L2, Left, **X**, R1, L1, Right, **X**.

Cars Don't Stop

Press R2, **●**, R1, L2, Left, R1, L1, R2, L2.

Pedestrians Riot

Press Down, Left, Up, Left, **X**, R2, R1, L2, L1.

Pedestrians Attack

Press Down, Up, Up, Up, **X**, R2, R1, L2, L2.

Pedestrians Have Weapons

Press R2, R1, **X**, **▲**, **X**, **▲**, Up, Down.

Women with Guns

Press Right, L1, **●**, L2, Left, **X**, R1, L1, L1, **X**.

Women Follow You

Press **●**, **X**, L1, L1, R2, **X**, **X**, **●**, **▲**.

Media Level Meter

Press R2, **●**, Up, L1, Right, R1, Right, Up, **■**, **▲**.

Weapon Cheats

The following will give you one weapon for each weapon class:

Weapons Set 1

Press R2, R2, R1, R2, L1, R2, Left, Down, Right, Up, Left Down, Right, Up.

Weapons Set 2

Press R1, R2, L1, R2, Left, Down, Right, Up, Left, Down, Down, Left.

Weapons Set 3

Press R1, R2, L1, R2, Left, Down, Right, Up, Left, Down, Down, Down.

Weather Cheats

Change the weather with the following cheats:

Clear

Press R2, **X**, L1, L1, L2, L2, L2, Down.

Sunny

Press R2, **X**, L1, L1, L2, L2, L2, ▲.

Overcast

Press R2, **X**, L1, L1, L2, L2, L2, ■.

Rain

Press R2, **X**, L1, L1, L2, L2, L2, ●.

Fog

Press R2, **X**, L1, L1, L2, L2, L2, **X**.

Appearance Cheats

The following change Tommy's appearance to the indicated character:

Red Leather

Press Right, Right, Left, Up, L1, L2, Left, Up, Down, Right.

Candy Suxxx

Press ●, R2, Down, R1, Left, Right, R1, L1, **X**, L2.

Hilary King

Press R1, ●, R2, L1, Right, R1, L1, **X**, R2.

Ken Rosenberg
Press Right, L1, Up, L2, L1, Right, R1, L1, **X**, R1.

Lance Vance
Press ●, L2, Left, **X**, R1, L1, **X**, L1.

Love Fist 1
Press Down, L1, Down, L2, Left, **X**, R1, L1, **X**, **X**.

Love Fist 2
Press R1, L2, R2, L1, Right, R2, Left, **X**, ■, L1.

Mercedes
Press R2, L1, Up, L1, Right, R1, Right, Up, ●, ▲.

Phil Cassady
Press Right, R1, Up, R2, L1, Right, R1, L1, Right, ●.

Ricardo Diaz

Press L1, L2, R1, R2, Down, L1, R2, L2.

Sonny Forelli

Press ●, L1, ●, L2, Left, **X**, R1, L1, **X**, **X**.

Vehicle Cheats

The following vehicles will drop from the sky:

Bloodring Banger

Press Up, Right, Right, L1, Right, Up, ■, L2.

Bloodring Banger

Press Down, R1, ●, L2, L2, **X**, R1, L1, Left, Left.

Caddy

Press ●, L1, Up, R1, L2, **X**, R1, L1, ●, **X**.

Hotring Racer

Press R2, L1, ●, Right, L1, R1, Right, Up, ●, R2.

Hotring Racer

Press R1, ●, R2, Right, L1, L2, **X**, **X**, ■, R1.

Love Fist Limo

Press R2, Up, L2, Left, Left, R1, L1, ●, Right.

Rhino Tank

Press ●, ●, L1, ●, ●, ●, L1, L2, R1, ▲, ●, ▲.

Sabre Turbo

Press Right, L2, Down, L2, L2, **X**, R1, L1, ●, Left.

Romero's Hearse

Press Down, R2, Down, R1, L2, Left, R1, L1, Left, Right.

Trashmaster

Press ●, R1, ●, R1, Left, Left, R1, L1, ●, Right.

HIGH HEAT MAJOR LEAGUE BASEBALL 2004

Ball Cannon and Game State Options

Pause the game and press ■, ■, ●, ●, L1, R1. Then, press L1 + L2 + R1 + R2.

HITMAN 2: SILENT ASSASSIN

Level Select

At the Main menu, press R2, L2, Up, Down, ■, ▲, ●.

Complete Level

During a game, press R2, L2, Up, Down, **X**, L3, ●, **X**, ●, **X**.

All Weapons

During a game, press R2, L2, Up, Down, **X**, Up, ■, **X**.

Invincibilty

During a game, press R2, L2, Up, Down, **X**, R2, L2, R1, L1.

Full Heal

During a game, press R2, L2, Up, Down, **X**, Up, Down.

Toggle Lethal Charge

During a game, press R2, L2, Up, Down, **X**, R1, R1.

Gravity

During a game, press R2, L2, Up, Down, **X**, L2, L2.

Slow Motion

During a game, press R2, L2, Up, Down, **X**, Up, L2.

Megaforce

During a game, press R2, L2, Up, Down, **X**, R2, R2.

Toggle Bomb Mode

During a game, press R2, L2, Up, Down, **X**, Up, L1.

Toggle Punch Mode

During a game, press R2, L2, Up, Down, **X**, Up, Up.

Toggle Nailgun Mode

During a game, press R2, L2, Up, Down, **X**, L1, L1.

HOT WHEELS: VELOCITY X

All Cars and Tracks

At the Main menu, hold R1 + L1 and press ●, ■, ■, ▲, X.

JAMES BOND 007: NIGHTFIRE

Select Codenames from the Main menu and select your codename. Select Secret Unlocks and enter the following codes. Save your codename before backing out of this menu.

Level Select
Enter PASSPORT.

Alpine Escape Level
Enter POWDER.

Enemies Vanquished Level
Enter TRACTION.

Double Cross Level
Enter BONSAI.

Night Shift Level
Enter HIGHRISE.

Chain Reaction Level
Enter MELTDown.

Countdown Level
Enter BLASTOFF.

Equinox Level
Enter VACUUM.

All Gadget Upgrades
Enter Q LAB.

Camera Upgrade
Enter SHUTTER.

Decrypter Upgrade
Enter SESAME.

Grapple Upgrade
Enter LIFTOFF.

Laser Upgrade
Enter PHOTON.

Scope Upgrade
Enter SCOPE.

Phoenix Fire Level
Enter FLAME.

Deep Descent Level
Enter AQUA.

Island Infiltration Level
Enter PARADISE.

Stunner Upgrade
Enter ZAP.

Tranquilizer Dart Upgrade
Enter SLEEPY.

Bigger Clip for Sniper Rifle
Enter MAGAZINE.

P2K Upgrade
Enter P2000.

Golden Wolfram P2K
Enter AU P2K.

Golden PP7
Enter AU PP7.

Vanquish Car Missile Upgrade
Enter LAUNCH.

All Multiplayer Scenarios
Enter GAMEROOM.

Uplink Multiplayer Scenario

Enter TRANSMIT.

Demolition Multiplayer Scenario

Enter TNT.

Protection Multiplayer Scenario

Enter GUARDIAN.

GoldenEye Strike Multiplayer Scenario

Enter ORBIT.

Assassination Multiplayer Scenario

Enter TARGET.

Team King of the Hill Multiplayer Scenario

Enter TEAMWORK.

Explosive Scenery Option in Multiplayer

Enter BOOM. Find this option in the Enviro-Mods menu.

All Characters in Multiplayer

Enter PARTY.

Play as Bond Tux in Multiplayer

Enter BLACKTIE.

Play as Drake Suit in Multiplayer

Enter NUMBER 1.

Play as Bond Spacesuit in Multiplayer

Enter ZERO G.

Play as Goldfinger in Multiplayer

Enter MIDAS.

Play as Renard in Multiplayer

Enter HEADCASE.

Play as Scaramanga in Multiplayer

Enter ASSASSIN.

Play as Christmas Jones in Multiplayer

Enter NUCLEAR.

Play as Wai Lin in Multiplayer

Enter MARTIAL.

Play as Xenia Onatopp in Multiplayer

Enter JANUS.

Play as May Day in Multiplayer

Enter BADGIRL.

Play as Elektra King in Multiplayer

Enter SLICK.

Play as Jaws in Multiplayer

Enter DENTAL.

Play as Baron Samedi in Multiplayer

Enter VOODOO.

Play as Oddjob in Multiplayer

Enter BOWLER.

Play as Nick Nack in Multiplayer

Enter BITESIZE.

Play as Max Zorin in Multiplayer

Enter BLIMP.

Drive an SUV on Enemies Vanquished Level

Start the Enemies Vanquished Level and pause the game. Hold L1 and press ■, ●, ▲, ■, ▲, then release L1.

Race the Enemies Vanquished Level in Cobra

Start the Enemies Vanquished Level and pause the game. Hold L1 and press ●, ●, ■, ■, ▲, then release L1.

Enter the following during a driving level:

Faster Racing

Pause the game, hold L1 and press ■, ▲, ●, ■, ▲, ●, then release L1.

Berserk Racing

Pause the game, hold L1 and press ■, ▲, ▲, ■, ▲, ●, then release L1.

Trails During Racing

While racing on the Paris Prelude, Enemies Vanquished, Island Infiltration, or Deep Descent level, press START to pause the game, then hold L1 and press ■, ●, ●, ■, then release L1.

Double Armor During Racing

While racing on the Paris Prelude, Enemies Vanquished, Island Infiltration, or Deep Descent level, press START to pause the game, then hold L1 and press ■, ▲, ●, ■, ■, then release L1.

Triple Armor During Racing

While racing on the Paris Prelude, Enemies Vanquished, Island Infiltration, or Deep Descent level, press START to pause the game, then hold L1 and press ■, ▲, ●, ■ (x3), then release L1.

Quadruple Armor During Racing

While racing on the Paris Prelude, Enemies Vanquished, Island Infiltration, or Deep Descent level, press START to pause the game, then hold L1 and press ■, ▲, ●, ■ (x4), then release L1.

Super Bullets During Racing

While racing on the Paris Prelude, Enemies Vanquished, Island Infiltration, or Deep Descent level, press START to pause the game, then hold L1 and press ● (x4), then release L1. Note: This can also be done when you are flying the plane with Alura.

JURASSIC PARK: OPERATION GENESIS

Gimme Some Money

During a game, press L1, Up, L1, Down, L1. This will give you $10,000.

Where's the Money?

During a game, press R1, L1, Down. This will take all of your money away.

Impossible Mission

During a game, press R1, Left, Left, Left, Left, R1. This will give you all missions complete.

Rampage Time

During a game, press L1, L1, L1, Left, Left, Left. With this cheat, all carnivores will rampage.

Extinction Event

During a game, press L1, R1, Down, R1, L1. This will kill all dinosaurs.

Oh No!

During a game, hold R1 and press Right, Left, Right, Left, Right. This will kill all visitors.

Dial-A-Twister

During a game, press Left, Up, Right, Down, L1, R1.

No Twisters

During a game, hold L1 + R1, press Left, Right, then press R1, L1.

Hot One

During a game, hold R1 and press Down, Down. This will cause a heat wave.

Welcome to Melbourne

During a game, press R1, R1, L1, R1, Down, Up, Down. This will cause rainstorms.

Guaranteed Immunity

During a game, hold L1 and press R1, Up, Up. Dinosaurs won't get sick with this cheat.

No Red Tape

During a game, press L1, R1, Left, Down, Down, Down. With this cheat, you will not get charged for deaths.

Open to the Public

During a game, press Left, Down, Right, Up, L1, R1, L1, R1. This gives you the selection of dig sites without the required stars.

Market Day

During a game, press R1, L1, Down, R1, L1, Down.

equencing Error

During a game, press Down, R1, Up. This gives 55% dinosaur genomes.

Drive By

During a game, press R1, L1, Left, Down, Right, Right. Safari ride camera acts like a gun.

Crash

During a game, old R1 + L1 and press Up, Down, Up, Down.

Isla Muerta

During a game, press R1, R1, R1, L1, Right. Dinosaurs will appear decayed.

MAT HOFFMAN'S PRO BMX 2

Level Select

At the Title screen, press ■, Right, Right, ▲, Down, ■. This works for Session, Free Ride, and Multiplayer modes.

Boston, MA Level (Road Trip)

At the Title screen, press ■, Up, Down, Down, Up, ■.

Chicago, IL Level (Road Trip)

At the Title screen, press ■, Up, ▲, Up, ▲, ■.

Las Vegas, NV Level (Road Trip)

At the Title screen press ■, R1, Left, L1, Right, ■.

Los Angeles, CA Level (Road Trip)

At the Title screen, press ■, Left, ▲, ▲, Left, ■.

New Orleans, LA Level (Road Trip)

At the Title screen, press ■, Down, Right, Up, Left, ■.

Portland, OR Level (Road Trip)

At the Title screen, press ■, X, X, ▲, ▲, ■.

Day Smith

At the Title screen, press ▲, Up, Down, Up, Down, ■.

Vanessa

At the Title screen, press ▲, Down, Left, Left, Down, ■.

Big Foot

At the Title screen, press ▲, Right, Up, Right, Up, ■.

The Mime

At the Title screen, press ▲, Left, Right, Left, Right, Left.

Volcano

At the Title screen, press ▲, Up, Up, **X**, Up, Up, **X**.

Elvis Costume

At the Title screen, press ●, LI, LI, Up, Up.

BMX Costume

At the Title screen, press ●, ▲, Left, Right, Left, ●.

Tiki Battle Mode

At the Title screen, press LI, LI, Down, RI, **X**, LI.

Mat Hoffman Videos

At the Title screen, press RI, Left, ●, Left, ●, Left, RI.

Joe Kowalski Videos

At the Title screen, press RI, Up, **X**, ▲, Down, RI.

Rick Thorne Videos

At the Title screen, press RI, LI, Right, RI, Left, RI.

Mike Escamilla Videos

At the Title screen, press RI, I, **X**, **X**, ●, **X**, **X**, RI.

Simon Tabron Videos

At the Title screen, press RI, LI, LI, RI, LI, LI, RI.

Kevin Robinson Videos

At the Title screen, press RI, **X**, ▲, Down, Up, RI.

Cory Nastazio Videos

At the Title screen, press RI, ■, ●, ●, ■ (x3), RI.

Ruben Alcantara Videos

At the Title screen, press RI, Left, Right, Left, Right, Left, Right, RI.

Seth Kimbrough Videos

At the Title screen, press RI, Up, Up, ● (x3), RI.

Nate Wessel Videos

At the Title screen, press RI, Down, ▲, ●, Down, ▲, ●, RI.

Big Ramp Video

At the Title screen, press RI, Up, Down, Left, **X**, **X**, **X**, RI.

Day Flatland Video

At the Title screen, press RI, I, Left, Left, ■, Right, Right, RI.

All Music

At the Title screen, press LI, Left, Left, Right (x3), **X**, **X**.

MIDNIGHT CLUB II

Select Cheat Codes from the Options and enter the following:

All Vehicles

Enter theCollector.

All Cities, Vehicles, and Career in Arcade Mode

Enter pennyThug or rimbuk.

All Cities in Arcade Mode

Enter Globetrotter.

Weapons

Enter savethekids. Use L3 and R3 to fire.

Weapons and Invulnerability

Enter immortal.

Unlimited Nitrous in Arcade Mode

Enter greenLantern.

No Damage in Arcade Mode

Enter gladiator.

Better Air Control

Enter carcrobatics.

Change Difficulty

Enter one of the following. 0 is easiest, 9 is hardest.

howhardcanitbe0

howhardcanitbe1

howhardcanitbe2

howhardcanitbe3

howhardcanitbe4

howhardcanitbe5

howhardcanitbe6

howhardcanitbe7

howhardcanitbe8

howhardcanitbe9

MINORITY REPORT

Select Cheats from the Special menu and enter the following

Invincibility

Enter LRGARMS.

Level Warp All

Enter PASSKEY.

Level Skip

Enter QUITER.

All Combos

Enter NINJA.

All Weapons

Enter STRAPPED.

Infinite Ammo

Enter MRJUAREZ.

Super Damage

Enter SPINACH.

Health

Enter BUTTERUp.

Select Alternate Heroes from the Special menu to find the following:

Clown Hero
Enter SCARYCLOWN.

Convict Hero
Enter JAILBREAK.

GI John Hero
Enter GNRLIN-FANTRY.

Lizard Hero
Enter HISSSS.

Moseley Hero
Enter HAIRLOSS.

Zombie Hero
Enter IAMSODEAD.

Free Aim
Enter FPSSTYLE.

Pain Arenas
Enter MAXMUMHURT.

Nara Hero
Enter WEIGHTGAIN.

Nikki Hero
Enter BIGLIPS.

Robot Hero
Enter MRROBOTO.

Super John Hero
Enter SUPERJOHN.

Armor
Enter STEELUP.

Baseball Bat
Enter SLUGGER.

Rag Doll
Enter CLUMSY.

Slomo Button
Enter SLIZOMIZO.

Bouncy Men
Enter BOUNZMEN.

Wreck the Joint
Enter CLUTZ.

Dramatic Finish
Enter STYLIN.

Ending
Enter WIMP.

Concept Art
Enter SKETCHPAD.

All Movies

Enter DIRECTOR.

Do Not Select

Enter DONOTSEL.

MLB 2004

Big Ball

Pause the game and press L1, L2, L1, L2, Up, Right, Down, Left.

Big Bodies

Pause the game and press Up, Down, Left, Right, L1, L2, R2, R1.

No Bodies

Pause the game and press R1, R2, R1, R2, Up, Down, Left, Right.

Big Heads

Pause the game and press Up, Left, Down, Right, Up, Right, Down, Left.

Small Heads

Pause the game and press Up, Down, Up, Down, R1, R1, L1, L1.

Fast Players

Pause the game and press Left, Right, Right, Left, L1, R1, R1, L1.

Programmer Names

Pause the game and press R1, R2, Right, Right, Left, Left, L2, L1.

Slow Players

Pause the game and press Left, Left, Right, Right, R2, R2, L2, L2.

MLB SLUGFEST 20-04

Cheats

At the Match-Up screen, use ■, ▲ and ● to enter the following codes, then press the appropriate direction. For example, for "16" Softball" press ■ two times, ▲ four times, ● two times, then press Up.

Code	Enter
Cheats Disabled	111 Down
Unlimited Turbo	444 Down
16" Softball	242 Down
Whiffle Bat	004 Right

Big Head	200 Right
Log Bat	004 Up

Code	Enter
Ice Bat	003 Up
Blade Bat	002 Up
Spike Bat	005 Up
Bone Bat	001 Up
Coliseum Stadium	333 Up
Rocket Park Stadium	321 Up
Monument Stadium	333 Down

Midway Park Stadium	321 Down
Empire Park Stadium	321 Right
Forbidden City Stadium	333 Left
Atlantis Stadium	321 Left
Rubber Ball	242 Up
Mace Bat	004 Left
Tiny Head	200 Left
Max Batting	300 Left
Max Power	030 Left
Max Speed	003 Left
Pinto Team	210 Right
Horse Team	211 Right
Eagle Team	212 Right
Lion Team	220 Right

Code	Enter
Team Terry Fitzgerald	333 Right
Team Todd McFarlane	222 Right
Dwarf Team	103 Down
Gladiator Team	113 Down
Bobble Head Team	133 Down
Dolphin Team	102 Down
Scorpion Team	112 Down
Rodeo Clown	132 Down
Little League	101 Down
Minotaur Team	110 Down
Olshan Team	222 Down
Rivera Team	222 Up
Napalitano Team	232 Down
Evil Clown Team	211 Down

Alien Team	231 Down
Casey Team	233 Down
Extended Time For Codes	303 Up

MVP BASEBALL 2003

Broken Bats

Create a player named Keegn Patersn, Jacob Patersn, or Ziggy Patersn.

Home Run Cheat

Create a player named Erik Kiss.

NASCAR: DIRT TO DAYTONA

Master Code

At the Title screen, press R1, R1, Up, Down, R2, R2, Left, Right.

NBA 2K3

Codes

Select Game Play from the Options menu, hold Left on the D-pad + Right on the Left Analog Stick and press START. Back out to the Options, and a Codes option should appear.

Street Trash

Enter SPRINGER as a code.

NBA LIVE 2003

Select Roster Management from the Team Management menu. Create a player with the following last names. These characters will be available as free agents.

B-Rich
Enter DOLLABILLS.

Fabolous
Enter GHETTOFAB.

Busta Rhymes
Enter FLIPMODE.

Hot Karl
Enter CALIFORNIA.

DJ Clue
Enter MIXTAPES.

Just Blaze
Enter GOODBEATS.

NBA STARTING FIVE

Big Heads
Enter BIGHEAD as a code.

Big Feet
Enter BIGFOOT as a code.

Big Hands
Enter BIGHAND as a code.

Flat Players
Enter PANCAKE as a code.

First Pick at Draft
Enter FIRSTPICK as a code.

Red, White and Blue Hats
Enter SILKHAT as a code.

Glasses with Nose and Mustache
Enter PARTYGLASSES as a code.

NBA STREET VOL. 2

Select Pick Up Game, hold L1 and enter the following when it says "Enter cheat codes now" at the bottom of the screen:

Unlimited Turbo
Press ■, ■, ▲, ▲.

ABA Ball
Press ●, ■, ●, ■.

WNBA Ball
Hold L1 and press ●, ▲, ▲, ●

No Display Bars
Press ■, ● (x3).

All Jerseys
Press ■, ▲, ●, ●.

All Courts

Press ■, ▲, ▲, ■.

St. Lunatics Team and All Street Legends

Press ■, ▲, ●, ▲.

All NBA Legends

Press ■, ▲, ▲, ●.

Classic Michael Jordan

Press ■, ▲, ■ ■.

Explosive Rims

Press ● (x3), ▲.

Small Players

Press ▲, ▲, ●, ■.

Big Heads

Press ●, ■, ■, ●.

No Counters

Press ▲, ▲, ●, ●.

Ball Trails

Press ▲, ▲, ▲, ■.

All Quicks

Press ▲, ●, ▲, ■.

Easy Shots

Press ▲, ●, ■, ▲.

Hard Shots

Press ▲, ■, ●, ▲.

PRIMAL

Magic Codes

At the Main, Options, or Bonus Materials menu, hold L1 + L2 + R1 + R2 until the Magic Codes menu appears. Hold **X** on a letter and press Left or Right to change that letter. Once you have entered one of the following, press ■ to accept the code. Press ▲ to go back to the previous menu.

Invulnerable	MONSTROUS
Bonus B	PRIMAL
Bonus C	DEMONREALMS
Bonus D	MORTALIS
Bonus E	OBLIVION

PRO RACE DRIVER

Enter the following codes at the Bonus screen:

Realistic Handling

Enter SIM.

Enhanced Damage

Enter DAMAGE.

Credits

Enter CREDITS.

RATCHET AND CLANK

Defeat Drek, and then at the Goodies screen do the following:

Big Head Mode (Clank)

Flip Back, Hyper-Strike, Comet-Strike, Double Jump, Hyper-Strike, Flip Left, Flip Right, Full Second Crouch.

Big Head Mode (Enemies)

Stretch Jump, Flip Back, Flip Back, Flip Back, Stretch Jump, Flip Back, Flip Back, Flip Back, Stretch Jump, Flip Back, Flip Back, Flip Back, Full Second Crouch.

Big Head Mode (Non-Player Characters)

Flip Left, Flip Right, Flip Back, Flip Back, Comet-Strike, Double Jump, Comet-Strike, Hyper-Strike.

Big Head Mode (Ratchet)

Flip Back, Flip Back, Flip Back, Full Second Crouch, Stretch Jump, Full Second Glide.

Health at Max Gives Temporary Invincibility

Comet-Strike (x4), Flip Back, Full Second Crouch, Flip Back, Full Second Crouch, Comet-Strike (x4).

Mirrored Levels

Flip Left, Flip Left, Flip Left, Flip Left, 3-Hit Wrench Combo, Hyper Strike, Double Flip Right, Flip Right, Flip Right, Double Jump, Full Second Crouch.

Trippy Trails

Wall Jump (x10), Double Jump, Hyper-Strike.

RAYMAN ARENA

After entering one of the names listed here, press L2 + ● + ■ to enter it.

All Characters
Enter PUPPETS.

All Skins
Enter CARNIVAL.

All Levels
Enter ALLRAYMANM.

All Battle Levels
Enter ALLFISH.

All Race Levels
Enter ALLTRIBES.

Old TV Screen
Enter OLDTV.

Mode I Levels
Enter FIELDS.

Mode I Battle Levels
Enter ARENAS.

Mode I Race Levels
Enter TRACKS.

3D Mode
Enter 3DVISION.

ROCKY

Punch Double Damage

At the Main menu, hold R1 and press Right, Down, Left, Up, Left, L1.

Double Speed Boxing

At the Main menu, hold R1 and press Down, Left, Down, Up, Right, L1.

All Default Boxers and Arenas

At the Main menu, hold R1 and press Right, Down, Up, Left, Up, L1. Note: This does not unlock Mickey or the Rocky Statue.

All Default Boxers, Arenas, and Rocky Statue

At the Main menu, hold R1 and press Right (x3), Left, Right, L1.

All Default Boxers, Arenas, Rocky Statue, and Mickey

At the Main menu, hold R1 and press Up, Down, Down, Left, Left, L1.

Full Stats In Tournament and Exhibition Modes

At the Main menu, hold R1 and press Left, Up, Up, Down, Right, L1.

Full Stats in Movie Mode

At the Main menu, hold R1 and press Right, Down, Down, Up, Left, L1.

Win Fight in Movie Mode

At the Main menu, hold R1 and press Right, Right, Left, Left, Up, L1. During a fight, press R2 + L2 to win.

RUN LIKE HELL

Cheats

At the Inventory screen, press L1 + L2 + L3 + R1 + R2 + R3. Then enter the following:

Code	Enter
Refill Health	Up, Down, Up, Down, Left, Right, Left, Right, X, ●
Refill Armor	■, ●, X, ▲, ●, ■, ▲, X, L3, R3
Music Video	Left, Left, Left, ●, ●, X, L1, L1, R1, Up

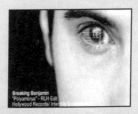

Code	Enter
Credits	X, ■, ▲, ●, Right, Up, Left, Up, X, Up

Max Damage (rifle)	L3, L3, L3, ■, ▲, ●, X, R3, R3, R3
Max Damage (pulse)	Left, Right, ●, Down, Left, X, Down, Up, X, ▲
Max Damage (shotgun)	X, X, X, X, L3, R3, Up, Down, Left, Right
Max Damage (repeater)	Left, ▲, Right, X, Up, ■, Down, ●, R3, L3
Max Damage (assault)	Left, ●, Right, ■, Down, ▲, Up, X, L3, R3
Max Damage (bolt toss)	X, ■, ▲, ●, X, ●, ▲, ■, X, Up

SEEK AND DESTROY

Enter the following passwords at the pink tank in the first town:

1000 Gold
Enter KWNOHIRO.

Boundbomb Weapon
Enter KKHWEEEE.

AirGatling Weapon
Enter GSASINRI.

Grand Flag
Enter ODGRITRO.

SHOX

$2,500,000

Start a new game in single-player mode and enter LOADED as a name.

SIMPSONS SKATEBOARDING

At the Character select, hold L1 + L2 + R1 + R2 and enter the following:

All Boards
Press X, ▲, ●, ■.

Level Select
Press ▲, X, ■, ●.

99 Dollars
Press ▲, X, ●, ■.

All Skaters
Press ●, ▲, X, ■.

Fuzzy Skaters
Press X, ▲, ■, ●.

Big Head Homer
Press ●, X, ▲, ■.

Underwear Homer
Press ▲, ●, X, ■.

Big Head Bart
Press X, ■, ●, ▲.

Gangsta Bart
Press ●, X, ■, ▲.

Demon Marge
Press X, ■, ▲, ●.

Big Head Lisa
Press ■, ▲, X, ●.

Gangsta Lisa
Press ■, ▲, ●, X.

Big Head Nelson
Press ▲, ■, ●, X.

Ballerina Nelson
Press ▲, ■, X, ●.

Sunglasses Otto
Press ■, X, ●, ▲.

Big Head Frink
Press ■, X, ▲, ●.

Groovy Frink
Press X, ●, ▲, ■.

Business Suit Krusty
Press ●, ▲, ■, X.

Big Head Chief Wiggum
Press X, ●, ■, ▲.

Man Eater Wiggum
Press ▲, ●, ■, X.

SOCCER SLAM

Max Power
At the Title screen, press L1, R1, Left, Right, ■, ■.

Infinite Turbo
At the Title screen, press L1, R1, Right, Up, ●, ●.

Big Heads
At the Title screen, press R1, L1, Up, Up, ■, ■.

Big Hit Mode
At the Title screen, press L1, R1, Up, Up, ●, ■.

Infinite Spotlight
At the Title screen, press L1, R1, Down, Right, ■, ●.

Old School Ball
At the Title screen, press R1, Right, Left, Left, ■, ●.

Eyeball Ball
At the Title screen, press R1, Right, Down, Up, ●, ●.

Black Box Ball
At the Title screen, press R1, Left, Left, Down, ●, ●.

Kids Play Ball
At the Title screen, press R1, Right, Up, Down, ●, ■.

Earth Ball

At the Title screen, press R1, Right, Right, Left, ●, ●.

Kid's Block Ball

At the Title screen, press R1, Left, Right, Right, ■, ■.

Rusty Can Ball

At the Title screen, press R1, Left, Up, Up, ■, ■.

Beach Ball

At the Title screen, press R1, Right, Right, Down, ■, ●.

Crate Ball

At the Title screen, press R1, Left, Down, Right, ■, ●.

Eight Ball

At the Title screen, press R1, Right, Up, Up, ■, ■

Rob Willock's Head Ball

At the Title screen, press R1, Left, Up, Left, ■, ●.

All Stadiums

At the Title screen, press R1, R1, Right, Right, Up (x5), ●, ●.

Alpen Castle Stadium

At the Title screen, press Up (x3), Down, ●, ●.

Jungle Stadium

At the Title screen, press L1, R1, Up, Down, Left, Right, ●, ■.

Atoll Stadium

At the Title screen, press Up, Up, Left, Left, ■, ■.

Reactor Stadium

At the Title screen, press Up, Left, Left, Right, ●, ■.

Riviera Ruins Stadium

At the Title screen, press Up, Down, Down, Right, ■, ●.

Oasis Stadium

At the Title screen, press L1, R1, Up, Up, Down, Down, ●, ●.

All Items

At the Title screen, press Left, ●, Left, ●, Left.

SUPERMAN: SHADOW OF APOKOLIPS

Select Cheat Codes from the Options menu and enter the following:

Master Code

Enter MXYZPTLK.

Expert Mode

Enter BIZZARO.

Unlimited Health

Enter SMALLVILLE.

Unlimited Superpowers

Enter JOR EL.

All Movies

Enter LANA LANG.

All Biographies

Enter LARA.

TENCHU: WRATH OF HEAVEN

All Characters

At the Title screen, press L1, R2, L2, R1, Right, Left, L3, R3.

All Story Mode Missions

At the Mission Select, press L1, R1, L2, R2, Right, ■, L3, R3.

All Layouts

At the Mission Select, press R3, L3, R2, L2, R1, L1.

All Multiplayer Missions

At the Mission Select, press L1, R1, L2, R2, Right, ■, L3, R3.

Bonus Rikimaru stage

At the Title screen, press L1, Up, R1, Down, L2, Right, R2, Left.

Hidden Level

At the Title screen, press Up, Down, Right, Left, **X** (x3).

All Items

At the Items screen, hold R1+L1 and press Up, ■, ■, Left, ■, ■, Down, ■, ■, Right, ■, ■.

Increase Items

At the Items screen, hold R2 + L2 and press ■, ■, ■, Up, Left, Down, Right.

Unlimited Item Capacity

At the Items screen, hold L1 + L2 + R1 + R2 and press ■ (x3), Up, Left, Down, Right, ■, Up, Right, Down, Left.

Regain Health

Pause the game and press Up, Down, Right, Left, ■, ■, ■.

Toggle Special Abilities

Pause the game, hold
L1 + L2, and press Up,
Up, Down, Down.
Release L1 + L2 and
press ■, ■, R1, R2.

Add 100 Points

Pause the game, hold
L1 + R1, and press
Right, Right, Left, Left
on controller two.

Score and Time

Pause the game and
press Right, Right, Left,
Left on controller two.

THE GETAWAY

Enter the following during the opening movie:

Double Health

Press Up, Up, Left, Left,
Right, Right, ●, ●,
Down.

Unlimited Ammo/No Reload

Press Up, Down, Left,
Right, ▲, Up, Down,
Left, Right, ■.

Armored Car Weapon

Press Up, Down, Left,
Right, ■, ▲, ●. Press L3
to fire weapon.

Free Roam Mode and Credits

Press ▲ (x3), Left, ■,
▲ (x3), Left, ●.

THE LORD OF THE RINGS: THE TWO TOWERS

Health

Pause the game, hold R1 + R2 + L1 + L2, and press ▲, Down, **X**, Up.

Arrows

Pause the game, hold L1 + L2 + R1 + R2, and press **X**, Down, ▲, Up.

1000 Experience Points

Pause the game, hold R1 + R2 + L1 + L2, and press **X**, Down (x3).

Level 2 Skills

Pause the game, hold R1 + R2 + L1 + L2, and press ●, Right, ●, Right.

Level 4 Skills

Pause the game, hold R1 + R2 + L1 + L2, and press ▲, Up, ▲, Up.

Level 6 Skills

Pause the game, hold R1 + R2 + L1 + L2, and press ■, Left, ■, Left.

Level 8 Skills

Pause the game, hold R1 + R2 + L1 + L2, and press **X**, **X**, Down, Down.

Complete the game before entering the following codes:

Always Devastating

Pause the game, hold R1 + R2 + L1 + L2, and press ■, ■, ●, ●.

Small Enemies

Pause the game, hold R1 + R2 + L1 + L2, and press ▲, ▲, X, X.

All Upgrades

Pause the game, hold R1 + R2 + L1 + L2, and press ▲, ●, ▲, ●.

Invulnerable

Pause the game, hold R1 + R2 + L1 + L2, and press ▲, ■, X, ●.

Slow Motion

Pause the game, hold R1 + R2 + L1 + L2, and press ▲, ●, X, ■.

Unlimited Missile Weapons

Pause the game, hold R1 + R2 + L1 + L2, and press ■, ●, X, ▲.

THE POWERPUFF GIRLS: RELISH RAMPAGE

Refill All Life

During a game, press L2, R1, R2, L1, X, ▲, ●, ■, R2, L1, L2, R1.

Extra Chemical X Bottle

During a game, press X, X, ●, X, ●, L1, L1, X, X, ●, X, ●, L1, L1.

Refill Health

During a game, press L1, L2, L1, ■, R2, R1, R2.

Full Health

During a game, press L2, R1, R2, L1, X, ▲, ●, ■, R2, L1, L2, R1.

THE SIMS

At the Main menu, press L1 + R1 + L2 + R2, then enter the following cheats:

Play The Sims Mode, All 2-Player Games, Objects and Skins

Enter MIDAS. Select Get A Life and start a new game. Join Roxy in the hot tub, pause the game and quit.

All Objects Cost 0 Simoleans

Enter FREEALL.

Party Motel Two-Player Game

Enter PARTY M.

Play The Sims Mode

Enter SIMS.

First Person View

Enter FISH EYE. Press ● to toggle the view.

TIGER WOODS PGA TOUR 2003

Select Cheat Codes from the Options menu and enter the following:

All Golfers

Enter ALLTW3.

All Courses

Enter 14COURSES.

Super Tiger Woods

Enter SUNDAY.

Cedric "Ace" Andrews

Enter IAM#1.

Stuart Appleby

Enter ORANGES.

Notah Begay III

Enter NOTABLY.

Mark Calavecchia

Enter CALCULATE.

Stewart Cink

Enter SINK.

Dominic "The Don" Donatello

Enter GODFATHER.

Brad Faxon

Enter XON.

Jim Furyk

Enter THESWING.

Charles Howell III

Enter BANDPANTS.

Justin Leonard

Enter JUSTINTIME.

Solita Lopez

Enter SOLITARY1.

Hamish "Mulligan" McGregor
Enter MCRUFF.

Takeharu "Tsunami" Moto
Enter 2TON.

Kellie Newman
Enter COWGIRL.

Mark O' Meara
Enter TB.

Josey "Superstar" Scott
Enter SUPERSTAR.

Vijay Singh
Enter VJSING.

Steve Stricker
Enter SS.

Black Rock Cove Course
Use a memory card with a Tiger Woods PGA Tour 2002 saved game.

Val "Sunshine" Summers
Enter VALENTINE.

Melvin "Yosh" Tanigawa
Enter YOYOYO.

Ty Tryon
Enter TYNO.

TOM AND JERRY: WAR OF THE WHISKERS

Unlimited Health
Press X, ●, X, ▲, ▲, ■, ●, ▲.

Unlimited Ammunition
Press ●, ■, ●, ▲, X, ■, X, X.

TONY HAWK'S PRO SKATER 4

All Cheats

Select Cheat Codes from the Options and enter watch_me_xplode.

Eddie, Jango Fett and Mike Vallely

Select Cheat Codes from the Options and enter homielist.

Daisy

Select Cheat Codes from the Options and enter (o)(o).

Always Special

Select Cheat Codes from the Options and enter doasuper.

Perfect Manuals

Select Cheat Codes from the Options and enter mullenpower.

Perfect Rail

Select Cheat Codes from the Options and enter ssbsts.

Matrix Mode

Select Cheat Codes from the Options and enter nospoon.

Secret Created Skaters

Enter the following names for hidden created skaters

#$%@!

Aaron Skillman

Adam Lippmann

Andrew Skates

Andy Marchal

Angus

Atiba Jefferson

Danaconda

Dave Stohl

DDT

DeadEndRoad

Fritz

Gary Jesdanun

grjost

Henry Ji

Jason Uyeda

Jim Jagger

Ben Scott Pye

Big Tex

Brian Jennings

Captain Liberty

Chauwa Steel

Chris Peacock

ConMan

Danaconda

Dave Stohl

DDT

Joe Favazza

John Rosser

Jow

Kenzo

Kevin Mulhall

Kraken

Lindsey Hayes

Lisa G Davies

Little Man

Marilena Rixfor

Mat Hoffman

Matt Mcpherson

Maya's Daddy

Meek West

Mike Day

Mike Lashever

Mike Ward

Mr. Brad

Nolan Nelson

Parking Guy

Peasus

Pete Day

Pooper

Rick Thorne

Sik

Stacey D

Stacey Ytuarte

Team Chicken

Ted Barber

Todd Wahoske

Top Bloke

Wardcore

Zac ZiG Drake

TOTAL IMMERSION RACING

All Cars

Enter Loaded as a career name.

CART Car

Enter Downforce as a career name.

All Tracks

Enter Road Sweeps as a career name.

Low Gravity

Enter Feather as a career name.

Disable HUD

Enter No Dogs as a career name.

Slow Motion

Enter Poke as a career name.

Slow CPU Cars

Enter Walk It as a career name.

Extreme Difficulty

Enter Road Trip as a career name.

WAKEBOARDING UNLEASHED

At the Main menu, enter the following. You will get the corresponding message when entered correctly.

All Gaps

Message: WAKE-BOARDING ROYALTY

R1,L1,L2,R2, R1,L1,L2,R2, R1,L1,L2,R2, R1,L1,L2,R2

Boards 2 and 3

Message: YOU GOT ALL THE BOARDS ...OR DID YOU

Up, Up, Left, Left, Right, Right, Down, Down, Up, Left, Right, Down, Up, Left, Right, Down

All Levels

Message: TRAVEL VISA APPROVED

■, ■, ■, ■, ●, ●, ●, ●, ▲, ▲, ▲, ▲, ■, ●, ▲

WHIRL TOUR

All Characters and Levels

Press ▲, ■, ●, ▲, Down, Right, Up, Left, L1, L1, Right, Right, Down, Up, R1, ●, Left, ■, ■, Down.

All Default Levels

Press ■ (x3), L1, Right, Down, ▲, Up, Left, ●, ■, Down, Up, R1, L1, Down, Down.

All Bonus Levels

Press Up, Up, Down, Down, Left, Right, Left, Right, ■, ●, ▲.

All Race Levels

Press ■, ▲, ●, ■, L1, ●, R1, ▲, L1, ●, R1, ■.

All Extras Options

Press Left, Right, L1, R1, Down, Up, Right, Down, ●, ●, ▲, Right, R1.

Complete All Current Objectives

Press ●, ●, ■, ●, ●, ▲, ●, ●, L1, R1.

WHITEOUT

All Characters

At the Main menu, hold R1 + L1 and press Down, Down, Down, Down.

All Tracks, Snowmobiles and Riders

At the Main menu, hold R1 + L1 and press Right, Right, Right, Right.

All Courses

At the Main menu, hold R1 + L1 and press Up, Up, Up, Up.

All Parts

At the Main menu, hold L1 + R1 and press Left, Left, Left, Left.

10,000 Points

During a race, hold L2 + ▲ and press Right, Right, Up, Down.

Automatically Win Race

During a race, hold L2 + ▲ and press Up, Down, Left, Right.

Stamina Cheat

During a race, hold L2 + ▲ and press Right, Right, Left, Down.

Target Cheat

During a race, hold L2 + ▲ and press Down, Down, Left, Left.

X2: WOLVERINE'S REVENGE

Level Select and All Challenges

At the Main menu, press ▲, ●, ▲, ■, ▲, ●, L1 + R1.

All Costumes

At the Main menu, press ▲, ●, ▲, ■, ■, ■, L1 + L2.

All Cerebro Files and FMV Sequences

At the Main menu, press ▲, ●, ▲, ■, ■, ■, R1 + R2.

YU-GI-OH! THE DUELIST OF THE ROSES

Passwords

At the Build Deck screen, press R3 and enter the following passwords:

Number	Card	Password
#001	Seiyaryu	2H4D85J7
#019	Meteor Dragon	86985631
#042	Fairy's Gift	NVE7A3EZ
#043	Magician of Faith	GME1S3UM
#057	Left Arm of the Forbidden One	A5CF6HSH
#058	Exodia the Forbidden One	37689434
#146	Swordstalker	AH0PSHEB
#149	Greenkappa	YBJMCD6Z
#152	Tactical Warrior	054TC727
#191	Swordsman from a Foreign Land	CZ81UVGR
#478	Aqua Dragon	JXCB6FU7
#655	Ancient Tree of Enlightenment	EKJHQ109
#502	Barrel Dragon	GTJXSBJ7
#567	Beastking of the Swamps	QXNTQPAX
#291	Birdface	N54T4TY5

Number	Card	Password
#348	Dragon Seeker	81EZCH8B
#372	Mystical Capture Chains	NINDJMQ3
#458	Serpentine Princess	UMQ3WZUZ
#506	Blast Sphere	CZN5GD2X
#510	Robotic Knight	S5S7NKNH
#670	Fairy King Truesdale	YF07QVEZ
#674	Slate Warrior	73153736
#687	Mimicat	69YDQM85
#699	Dark Hole	UMJI0MQB
#702	Harpy's Feather Duster	8HJHQPNP
#732	Change of Heart	SBYDQM8B
#750	Earthshaker	Y34PNISV
#758	Elf's Light	E5G3NRAD
#765	Horn of the Unicorn	SI4FGKQI
#794	Crush Card	SRA7L5YR
#806	Gravity Bind	0HNFG9WX
#814	Goblin Fan	92886423
#825	Royal Decree	8TETQHEI
#829	Mirror Wall	53297534

ZONE OF THE ENDERS: THE 2ND RUNNER

Zoradius Mini Game

Fight Vic Viper in Boss Battle Mode. Pause the game and press Up, Up, Down, Down, Left, Right, Left, Right, L1, R1. The Mini Game will be available at the Extra Missions screen.

All Power-Ups in Zoradius Mini Game: All Power-Ups

Pause the game and press Up, Up, Down, Down, Left, Right, Left, Right, L1, R1.

PlayStation®

Contents

C-12: FINAL RESISTANCE

nvincible

Pause the game, hold L2, and press Up, Left, Down, Right, ▲, ■, X, ●.

All Weapons

Pause the game, hold L2, and press Up, Left, Right, Down, ▲, ■, ●, X.

Shield

Pause the game, hold L2, and press Up, Left, Right, ▲, ■, ●.

Infinite Ammo

Pause the game, hold L2, and press Down, Left, Right, X, ■, ●.

Secondary Weapon Attacks

Pause the game, hold L2, and press Up, Down, Left, Right, ▲, X, ■, ●.

Stealth Mode

Pause the game, hold L2, and press X, X, ■, ■, ▲, ▲, ●, ●, X, X.

DELTA FORCE: URBAN WARFARE

Cheat Menu

At the Main menu, press Select, Right, Up, Down, ●, Left, ■, ▲, ●.

FINAL FANTASY ORIGINS

FINAL FANTASY

The Tile Game

When you're on your ship, hold **X**, then press ● 55 times to bring up a sliding tile puzzle game called 15 Puzzle. The game tracks your best time and rewards you accordingly:

Under 6 Minutes: Potion

Under 4 Minutes: Antidote and Potion

Under 2 Minutes: Golden Needle, Antidote, and Potion

1st Place Finish: 10,000 Gil

2nd Place Finish: 5,000 Gil

3rd Place Finish: 2,000 Gil

FINAL FANTASY 2

Concentration Mini Game

After you obtain the Snowcraft, hold **X** and press ● 15-20 times to start a game of concentration. An easy way to earn the maximum reward of 40,000 Gil, an Elixir, and a Phoenix Down is to beat the first puzzle and note the locations of the pairs. Restart and quit the game 31 times. (Don't exit the game screen; just cancel immediately after starting a game.) Then, the thirty-second layout is the same as the first board.

HOOTERS ROAD TRIP

All Cars

At the Map screen, press Up, Down, Left, Right, R1, L1.

All Tracks

At the Map screen, press L1, R1, Right, Left, Down, Up.

NBA LIVE 2003

Select Roster Management from the Team Management menu. Create a player with the following last names. These characters will be available as free agents.

B-Rich
DOLLABILLS

Busta Rhymes
FLIPMODE

DJ Clue
MIXTAPES

Fabolous
GHETTOFAB

Hot Karl
CALIFORNIA

Just Blaze
GOODBEATS

RUGRATS STUDIO TOUR

Big Head
Select Tag Race or Diapies of Thunder. Pause the game and press ●, ■, ●, X.

STREAK: HOVERBOARD RACING

All Riders
Select Sierra for Freestyle in a 6-lap Time Trial. Besides Edge as blade 2, turn off other blades and start the race. Pause and quit the race. Then at the Rider Select, press ▲ and press Up, Down, L1, R2, R1, L2, ●, SELECT.

STUART LITTLE 2

Debug
At the Main menu, press Left, L1, L1, Right, R1, R1, Up, Down.

Invincibility
At the Main menu, press L2, ■, L1, ●, R2, ■, L1, ●.

Full Ammo
At the Main menu, ■, L1, R1, Up, ●, L2, R2, Down.

Level Select
At the Main menu, press R2, Left, Right, R1, L1, Up, Down, L2.

Flycam
At the Main menu, press Up, L1, Down, R1, R2, Down, L2, Up.

All Movies
At the Main menu, press Right, ●, ■, ■, R1, R2, Left, L2.

Gallery Movies
At the Main menu, press ●, L2, Left, R1, R2, Right, L1.

Infinite Lives
Pause the game, hold L1, and press ●, ●, ▲.

THE ITALIAN JOB

Enter the following at the Main menu, unless otherwise noted. Applause will indicate correct entry.

All Cheats

Press ▲, ●, ▲, ●, ▲, ■, ▲, ■.

All Missions in Italian Job Mode

Press ●, ●, ▲, ■, ■.

All Missions in Challenge Mode

Press ■, ■, ▲, ●, ●, ■, ▲, ●.

All Missions in Checkpoint Mode

Press ●, ■, ▲, ■, ▲, ■, ▲, ■, ●.

All Missions in Destructor Mode

Press ▲, ■, ■, ▲, ■, ■, ▲, ● (x3).

All Missions in Free Ride

Press ■, ▲, ■, ● (x3), ▲, ●.

Level Select

In Career mode, pause the game, hold R1 and press ▲, Left, Left, ▲, ●, Up, Up, ■.

TOMB RAIDER CHRONICLES

Unlimited Health, Ammo, and Weapons

While in the game, press SELECT to access your inventory screen. Highlight the Timex and enter the following:

Hold Up + R1 + L1 + L2 + R2, then press ▲.

Every Item for Your Level

While in the game, press SELECT to access your inventory screen. Highlight the Timex and enter the following:

Every Item for Your Level

While in the game, press SELECT to access your inventory screen. Highlight the Timex and enter the following:

Hold Down + R1 + L1 + L2 + R2 then press ▲.

This also gives you the Special Features option at the Main menu.

Start at Second Adventure

Highlight the New Game option at the Main menu and enter the following:

Hold L1 + Up then press **X** to start at the Russian Base.

Start at Third Adventure

Highlight the New Game option at the Main menu and enter the following:

Hold **L2** + Up then press **X** to start at the Black Isle.

Start at Fourth Adventure

Highlight the New Game option at the Main menu and enter the following:

Hold R1 + Up then press **X** to start at the Tower Block.

TONY HAWK'S PRO SKATER 4

Complete Current Objective

Pause the game, hold L1, and press ▲, Right, Up, **X**, Right, ●, Up, ▲, ■, Left, Up, **X**.

YU-GI-OH! FORBIDDEN MEMORIES

Passwords

Number	Card	Password
001	Blue Eyes White Dragon	89631139
002	Mystical Elf	15025844
003	Hitotsu-Me Giant	76184692
004	Baby Dragon	88819587
005	Ryu-Kishin	15303296
006	Feral Imp	41392891
007	Winged Dragon #1	87796900
008	Mushroom Man	14181608
009	Shadow Specter	40575313
010	Blackland Fire Dragon	87564352
011	Sword Arm of Dragon	13069066
012	Swamp Battleguard	40453765
013	Tyhone	72842870
014	Battle Steer	18246479
015	Flame Swordsman	45231177
016	Time Wizard	71625222
017	Right Leg of the Forbidden One	08124921
018	Left Leg of the Forbidden One	44519536
019	Right Arm of the Forbidden One	70903634
020	Left Arm of the Forbidden One	07902349
021	Exodia the Forbidden	33396948
022	Summoned Skull	70781052
023	The Wicked Worm Beast	06285791
024	Skull Servant	32274490
025	Horn Imp	69669405
026	Battle Ox	05053103
027	Beaver Warrior	32452818
028	Rock Ogre Grotto #1	68846917
029	Mountain Warrior	04931562
030	Zombie Warrior	31339260
031	Koumori Dragon	67724379
032	Two-headed King Rex	94119974
033	Judgeman	30113682
034	Saggi the Dark Clown	66602787

Number	Card	Password
035	Dark Magician	46986414
036	The Snake Hair	29491031
037	Gaia the Dragon Champion	66889139
038	Gaia the Fierce Knight	06368038
039	Curse of Dragon	28279543
040	Dragon Piper	55763552
041	Celtic Guardian	91152256
042	Illusionist Faceless Mage	28546905
043	Karbonala Warrior	54541900
044	Rogue Doll	91939608
045	Oscillo Hero #2	27324313
046	Griffore	53829412
047	Torike	80813021
048	Sangan	26202165
049	Big Insect	53606874
050	Basic Insect	89091579
051	Armored Lizard	15480588
052	Hercules Beatle	52584282
053	Killer Needle	88979991
054	Gokibore	15367030
055	Giant Flea	41762634
056	Larvae Moth	87756343
057	Great Moth	14141448
058	Kuriboh	40640057
059	Mammoth Graveyard	40374923
060	Great White	13429800
061	Wolf	49417509
062	Harpie Lady	76812113
063	Harpie Lady Sisters	12206212
064	Tiger Axe	49791927
065	Silver Fang	90357090
066	Kojikocy	01184620
067	Perfectly Ultimate Great Moth	48579379
068	Garoozis	14977074
069	Thousand Dragon	41462083
070	Fiend Kraken	77456781
071	Jellyfish	14851496
072	Cocoon of Evolution	40240595
073	Kairyu-Shin	76634149
074	Giant Soldier of Stone	13039848
075	Man-Eating Plant	49127943
076	Krokodilus	76512652
077	Grappler	02906250
078	Axe Raider	48305365

Number	Card	Password
079	Megazowler	75390004
080	Uraby	01784619
081	Crawling Dragon #2	38289717
082	Red-eyes B. Dragon	74677422
083	Castle of Dark Illusions	00062121
084	Reaper of the Cards	33066139
085	King of Yamimakai	69455834
086	Barox	06840573
087	Dark Chimera	32344688
088	Metal Guardian	68339286
089	Catapult Turtle	95727991
090	Gyakutenno Megami	31122090
091	Mystic Horseman	68516705
092	Rabid Horseman	94905343
093	Zanki	30090452
094	Crawling Dragon	67494157
095	Crass Clown	93889755
096	Armored Zombie	20277860
097	Dragon Zombie	66672569
098	Clown Zombie	92667214
099	Pumpking the King of Ghosts	29155212
100	Battle Warrior	55550921
101	Wings of Wicked Flames	92944626
102	Dark Mask	28933734
103	Job Change Mirror	55337339
104	Curtain of the Dark ones	22026707
105	Tomozaurus	46457856
106	Spirit of the Winds	54615781
107	Kagenigen	80600490
108	Graveyard and the Hand of Invitation	27094595
109	Goddess With the Third Eye	53493204
110	Hero of the East	89987208
111	Doma the Angel of Silence	16972957
112	The Witch that Feeds on Life	52367652
113	Dark Gray	09159938
114	White Magical Hat	15150365
115	Kamion Wizard	41544074
116	Nightmare Scorpion	88643173
117	Spirit of the Books	14037717
118	Supporter in the Shadows	41422426
119	Trial of Nightmares	77827521
120	Dream Clown	13215230
121	Sleeping Lion	40200834
122	Yamatano Dragon Scroll	76704943

Number	Card	Password
123	Dark Plant	13193642
124	Ancient Tool	49587396
125	Faith Bird	75582395
126	Orion the Battle King	02971090
127	Ansatsu	48365709
128	Lamoon	75850803
129	Nemuriko	90963488
130	Weather Control	37243151
131	Octoberser	74637266
132	The 13th Grave	00032864
133	Charubin the Fire Knight	37421579
134	Mystical Capture Chain	63515678
135	Fiend's Hand	52800428
136	Witty Phantom	36304921
137	Mystery Hand	62793020
138	Dragon Statue	09197735
139	Blue-eyed Silver Zombie	35282433
140	Toad Master	62671448
141	Spiked Snail	98075147
142	Flame Manipulator	34460851
144	Djinn the Watcher of the Wind	97843505
145	The Bewitching Phantom Thief	24348204
146	Temple of Skulls	00732302
147	Monster Egg	36121917
148	The Shadow Who Controls the Dark	63125616
149	Lord of the Lamp	99510761
150	Akihiron	36904469
151	Rhaintumdos of the Red Sword	62403074
152	The Melting Red Shadow	98898173
153	Dokuroize the Grim Reaper	25882881
154	Fire Reaper	53581214
155	Larvas	94675535
156	Hard Armor	20060230
157	Firegrass	53293545
158	Man Eater	93553943
159	Dig Beak	29948642
160	M-Warrior #1	56342351
161	M-Warrior #2	92731455
162	Tainted Wisdom	28725004
163	Lisark	55210709
164	Lord of Zemia	81618817
165	The Judgement Hand	28003512
166	Mysterious Puppeteer	54098121
167	Ancient Jar	81492226

Number	Card	Password
168	Darkfire Dragon	17881964
169	Dark King of the Abyss	53375573
170	Spirit of the Harp	80770678
171	Big Eye	16768387
172	Armaill	53153481
173	Dark Prisoner	89558090
174	Hurricail	15042735
175	Ancient Brain	42431843
176	Fire Eye	88435542
177	Monsturtle	15820147
178	Claw Reacher	41218256
179	Phantom Dewan	77603950
180	Arlownay	14708569
181	Dark Shade	40196604
182	Masked Clown	77581312
183	Lucky Trinket	03985011
184	Genin	49370026
185	Eyearmor	64511793
186	Fiend Reflection #2	02863439
187	Gate Deeg	49258578
188	Synchar	75646173
189	Fusionist	01641882
190	Akakieisu	38035986
191	Lala Li-Oon	09430387
192	Key Mace	01929294
193	Turtle Tiger	37313348
194	Terra the Terrible	63308047
195	Doron	36151751
196	Arma Knight	00756652
197	Mech Mole Zombie	63545455
198	Happy Lover	99030164
199	Penguin Knight	36039163
200	Petit Dragon	75356564
201	Frenzied Panda	98818516
202	Air Marmot of Nefariousness	75889523
203	Phantom Ghost	61201220
204	Mabarrel	98795934
205	Dorover	24194033
206	Twin Long Rods #1	60589682
207	Droll Bird	97973387
208	Petit Angel	38142739
209	Winged Cleaver	39175982
210	Hinotama Soul	96851799
211	Kaminarikozou	15510988
212	Meotoko	53832650

Number	Card	Password
213	Aqua Madoor	85639257
214	Kagemusha of the Blue Flame	15401633
215	Flame Ghost	58528964
216	Dryad	84916669
217	B. Skull Dragon	11901678
218	Two-mouth Darkruler	57305373
219	Solitude	84794011
220	Masked Sorcerer	10189126
221	Kumootoko	56283725
222	Midnight Fiend	83678433
223	Roaring Ocean Snake	19066538
224	Trap Master	46461247
225	Fiend Sword	22855882
226	Skull Stalker	54844990
227	Hitodenchak	46718686
228	Wood Remains	17733394
229	Hourglass of Life	08783685
230	Rare Fish	80516007
231	Wood Clown	17511156
232	Madjinn Gunn	43905751
233	Dark Titan of Terror	89494469
234	Beautiful Head Huntress	16899564
235	Wodan the Resident of the Forest	42883273
236	Guardian of the Labyrinth	89272878
237	Haniwa	84285623
238	Yashinoki	41061625
239	Vishwar Randi	78556320
240	The Drdek	08944575
241	Dark Assassin	41949033
242	Candle of Fate	47695416
243	Water Element	03732747
244	Dissolverock	40826495
245	Meda Bat	76211194
246	One Who Hunts Souls	03606209
247	Root Water	39004808
248	Master & Expert	75499502
249	Water Omotics	02483611
250	Hyo	38982356
251	Enchanting Mermaid	75376965
252	Nekogal #1	01761063
253	Angelwitch	37160778
254	Embryonic Beast	64154377
255	Prevent Rat	00549481
256	Dimensional Warrior	37043180
257	Stone Armadiller	63432835

Number	Card	Password
258	Beastking of the Swamp	99426834
259	Ancient Sorcerer	36821538
260	Lunar Queen Elzaim	62210247
261	Wicked Mirror	15150371
262	The Little Swordsman of Aile	25109950
263	Rock Ogre Grotto #2	62193699
264	Wing Egg Elf	98582704
265	The Furious Sea King	18710707
266	Princess of Tsurugi	51371017
267	Unknown Warrior of Fiend	97360116
268	Sectarian of Secrets	15507080
269	Versago the Destroyer	50259460
270	Wetha	96643568
271	Megirus Light	23032273
272	Mavelus	59036972
273	Ancient Tree of Enlightenment	86421986
274	Green Phantom King	22910685
275	Ground Attacker Bugroth	58314394
276	Ray & Temperature	85309439
277	Gorgon Egg	11793047
278	Petit Moth	58192742
279	King Fog	84686841
280	Protector of the Throne	10071456
281	Mystic Clown	47060154
282	Mystical Sheep #2	83464209
283	Holograph	10859908
284	Tao the Chanter	46247516
285	Serpent Maurauder	82742611
286	Gate Keeper	19737320
287	Ogre of the Black Shadow	45121025
288	Dark Arts	72520073
289	Change Slime	18914778
290	Moon Envoy	45909477
291	Fireyarou	71407486
292	Psychic Kappa	07892180
293	Masaki the Legendary Swordsman	44287299
294	Dragoness the Wiched Knight	70681994
295	Bio Plant	07670542
296	One-eyed Shield Dragon	33064647
297	Cyber Soldier of Dark World	75559356
298	Wicked Dragon with the Ersatz Head	02957055
299	Sonic Maid	38942059
300	Kurama	85705804
301	Legendary Sword	61854111
302	Sword of Dark Destruction	37120512

Number	Card	Password
303	Dark Energy	04614116
304	Axe of Dispair	40619825
305	Laser Cannon Armor	77007920
306	Insect Armor With A Laser Cannon	03492538
307	Elf's Light	39897277
308	Beast Fangs	46009906
309	Steel Shell	02370081
310	Vile Germs	39774685
311	Black Pendant	65169794
312	Silver Bow and Arrow	01557499
313	Horn of Light	38552107
314	Horn of the Unicorn	64047146
315	Dragon Treasure	01435851
316	Electro-Whip	37820550
317	Cyber Shield	63224564
318	Elegant Egotist	90219263
319	Mystical Moon	36607978
320	Stop Defense	63102017
321	Malevolent Nuzzeler	99597615
322	Violet Crystal	15052462
323	Book of Secret Arts	91595718
324	Invigoration	98374133
325	Machine Conversion Factory	25769732
326	Raise Body Heat	51267887
327	Follow Wind	98252586
328	Power of Kaishin	77027445
329	Dragon Capture Jar	50045299
330	Forest	87430998
331	Wasteland	23424603
332	Mountain	50913601
333	Sogen	86318356
334	Umi	22702055
335	Yami	59197169
336	Dark Hole	53129443
337	Raigeki	12580477
338	Mooyan Curry	58074572
339	Red Medicine	38199696
340	Goblin's Secret Remedy	11868825
341	Soul of the Pure	47852924
342	Dian Keto the Cure Master	84257639
343	Sparks	76103675
344	Hinotama	46130346
345	Final Flame	73134081
346	Ookazi	19523799

Number	Card	Password
347	Tremendose Fire	46918794
348	Swords of Revealing Light	72302403
349	Spellbinding Circle	18807108
350	Dark Piercing Light	45895206
351	Yaranzo	71280811
352	Kanan the Swordmistress	12829151
353	Takriminos	44073668
354	Stuffed Animal	71068263
355	Megasonic Eye	07562372
356	Super War-Lion	33951077
357	Yamadron	70345785
358	Seiyaryu	06740720
359	Three-Legged Zombie	33734439
360	Zera the Mant	69123138
361	Flying Penguin	05628232
362	Millennium Shield	32012841
363	Fairy's Gift	68401546
364	Black Luster Soldier	05405694
365	Fiend's Mirror	31890399
366	Labyrinth Wall	67284908
367	Jirai Gumo	94773007
368	Shadow Ghoul	30778711
369	Wall Shadow	63182310
370	Labyrinth Tank	99551425
371	Sanga of the Thunder	25955164
372	Kazejin	62340868
373	Suijin	98434877
374	Gate Guardian	25833572
375	Dungeon Worm	51228280
376	Monster Tamer	97612389
377	Ryu-Kishin Powered	24611934
378	Swordstalker	50005633
379	La Jinn the Mystical Genie	97590747
380	Blue Eyes Ultimate Dragon	23995346
381	Toon Alligator	59383041
382	Rude Kaiser	26378150
383	Parrot Dragon	62762898
384	Dark Rabbit	99261403
385	Bickuribox	25655502
386	Harpie's Pet Dragon	52040216
387	Mystic Lamp	98049915
388	Pendulum Machine	24433920
389	Giltia the D. Knight	51828629
390	Launcher Spider	87322377

Number	Card	Password
391	Zoa	24311372
392	Metalzoa	50705071
393	Zone Eater	86100785
394	Steel Scorpion	13599884
395	Dancing Elf	59983499
396	Ocubeam	86088138
397	Leghul	12472242
398	Ooguchi	58861941
399	Swordsman from the Foreign Land	85255550
400	Emperor of the Land and Sea	11250655
401	Ushi Oni	48649353
402	Monster Eye	84133008
403	Leogun	10538007
404	Tatsunootoshigo	47922711
405	Saber Slasher	73911410
406	Yaiba Robo	10315429
407	Machine King	46700124
408	Giant Mech-Soldier	72299832
409	Metal Dragon	09293977
410	Mechanical Spider	45688586
411	Bat	72076281
412	Giga-Tech Wolf	08471389
413	Cyber Soldier	44865098
414	Shovel Crusher	71950093
415	Mechanicalchacer	07359741
416	Blocker	34743446
417	Blast Juggler	70138455
418	Golgoil	07526150
419	Giganto	33621868
420	Cyber-Stein	69015963
421	Cyber Commander	06400512
422	Jinzo #7	32809211
423	Dice Armadillo	69893315
424	Sky Dragon	95288024
425	Thunder Dragon	31786629
426	Stone D.	68171737
427	Kaiser Dragon	94566432
428	Magician of Faith	31560081
429	Goddess of Whim	67959180
430	Water Magician	93343894
431	Ice Water	20848593
432	Waterdragon Fairy	66836598
433	Ancient Elf	93221206
434	Beautiful Beast Trainer	29616941

Number	Card	Password
435	Water Girl	55014050
436	White Dolphin	92409659
437	Deepsea Shark	28593363
438	Metal Fish	55998462
439	Bottom Dweller	81386177
440	7 Colored Fish	23771716
441	Mech Bass	50176820
442	Aqua Dragon	86164529
443	Sea King Dragon	23659124
444	Turu-Purun	59053232
445	Guardian of the Sea	85448931
446	Aqua Snake	12436646
447	Giant Red Snake	58831685
448	Spike Seadra	85326399
449	30,000-Year White Turtle	11714098
450	Kappa Avenger	48109103
451	Kanikabuto	84103702
452	Zarigun	10598400
453	Millennium Golem	47986555
454	Destroyer Golem	73481154
455	Barrel Rock	10476868
456	Minomushi Warrior	46864967
457	Stone Ghost	72269672
458	Kaminari Attack	09653271
459	Tripwire Beast	45042329
460	Bolt Escargot	12146024
461	Bolt Penguin	48531733
462	The Immortal of Thunder	84926738
463	Electric Snake	11324436
464	Wing Eagle	47319141
465	Punished Eagle	74703140
466	Skull Red Bird	10202894
467	Crimson Sunbird	46696593
468	Queen Bird	73081602
469	Armed Ninja	09076207
470	Magical Ghost	46474915
471	Soul Hunter	72869010
472	Air Eater	08353769
473	Vermillion Sparrow	35752363
474	Sea Kamen	71746462
475	Sinister Serpent	08131171
476	Ganigumo	34536276
477	Aliensection	70924884
478	Insect Soldiers of the Sky	07019529

479	Cockroach Knight	33413638
480	Kuwagata Alpha	60802233
481	Burglar	06297941
482	Pragtical	33691040
483	Garvas	69780745
484	Amoeba	95174353
485	Korogashi	32569498
486	Boo Koo	68963107
487	Flower Wolf	95952802
488	Rainbow Flower	21347810
489	Barrel Lily	67841515
490	Needle Ball	94230224
491	Peacock	20624263
492	Hoshinigen	67629977
493	Maha Vailo	93013676
494	Rainbow Marine Mermaid	29402771
495	Musicain King	56907389
496	Wilmee	92391084
497	Yado Karu	29380133
498	Morinphen	55784832
499	Kattapillar	81179446
500	Dragon Seeker	28563545
501	Man-Eater Bug	54652250
502	D. Human	81057959
503	Turtle Raccoon	17441953
504	Fungi of the Musk	53830602
505	Prisman	80234301
506	Gale Dogra	16229315
507	Crazy Fish	53713014
508	Cyber Saurus	89112729
509	Bracchio-Raidus	16507828
510	Laughing Flower	42591472
511	Bean Soldier	84990171
512	Cannon Soldier	11384280
513	Guardian of the Throne Room	47879985
514	Brave Scizzar	74277583
515	The Statue of Easter Island	10262698
516	Muka Muka	46657337
517	Sand Stone	73051941
518	Boulder Tortoise	09540040
519	Fire Kraken	46534755
520	Turtle Bird	72929454
521	Skullbird	08327462
522	Monstrous Bird	35712107

Number	Card	Password
523	The Bistro Butcher	71107816
524	Star Boy	08201910
525	Spirit of the Mountain	34690519
526	Neck Hunter	70084224
527	Milus Radiant	07489323
528	Togex	33878931
529	Flame Cerberus	60862676
530	Eldeen	06367785
531	Mystical Sand	32751480
532	Gemini Elf	69140098
533	Kwagar Hercules	95144193
534	Minar	32539892
535	Kamakiriman	68928540
536	Mechaleon	94412545
537	Mega Thunderball	21817254
538	Niwatori	07805359
539	Corroding Shark	34290067
540	Skelengel	60694662
541	Hanehane	07089711
542	Misairuzame	33178416
543	Tongyo	69572024
544	Dharma Cannon	96967123
545	Skelgon	32355828
546	Wow Warrior	69750536
547	Griggle	95744531
548	Bone Mouse	21239280
549	Frog the Jam	68638985
550	Behegon	94022093
551	Dark Elf	21417692
552	Winged Dragon #2	57405307
553	Mushroom Man #2	93900406
554	Lava Battleguard	20394040
555	Tyhone #2	56789759
556	The Wandering Doomed	93788854
557	Steel Ogre Grotto #1	29172562
558	Pot the Trick	55567161
559	Oscillo Hero	82065276
560	Invader from Another Planet	28450915
561	Lesser Dragon	55444629
562	Needle Worm	81843628
563	Wretched Ghost of the Attic	17238333
564	Great Mammoth of Goldfine	54622031
565	Man-Eating Black Shark	80727036
566	Yormungarde	17115745

Number	Card	Password
567	Darkworld Thorns	43500484
568	Anthrosaurus	89904598
569	Drooling Lizard	16353197
570	Trakadon	42348802
571	B. Dragon Jungle King	89832901
572	Empress Judge	15237615
573	Little D.	42625254
574	Witch of the Black Forest	78010363
575	Ancient One of the Deep Forest	14015067
576	Giant Scorpion of the Tundra	41403766
577	Crow Goblin	77998771
578	Leo Wizard	04392470
579	Abyss Flower	40387124
580	Patrol Robo	76775123
581	Takuhee	03170832
582	Dark Witch	35565537
583	Weather Report	72053645
584	Binding Chain	08058240
585	Mechanical Snail	34442949
586	Greenkappa	61831093
587	Mon Larvas	07225792
588	Living Vase	34320307
589	Tentacle Plant	60715406
590	Beaked Snake	06103114
591	Morphing Jar	33508719
592	Muse-A	69992868
593	Giant Turtle Who Feeds on Flames	96981563
594	Rose Spectre of Dunn	32485271
595	Fiend Reflection #1	68870276
596	Ghoul With An Appetite	95265975
597	Pale Beast	21263083
598	Little Chimera	68658728
599	Violent Rain	94042337
600	Key Mace #2	20541432
601	Tenderness	57935140
602	Penguin Soldier	93920745
603	Fairy Dragon	20315854
604	Obese Marmot of Nefariousness	56713552
605	Liquid Beast	93108297
606	Twin Long Rods #2	29692206
607	Great Bill	55691901
608	Shining Friendship	82085619
609	Bladefly	28470714
610	Electric Lizard	55875323

Number	Card	Password
611	Hiro's Shadow Scout	81863068
612	Lady of Faith	17358176
613	Twin-headed Thunder Dragon	54752875
614	Hunter Spider	80141480
615	Armored Starfish	17535588
616	Hourglass of Courage	43530283
617	Marine Beast	29929832
618	Warrior of Tradition	56413937
619	Rock Spirit	82818645
620	Snakeyashi	29802344
621	Succubus Knight	55291359
622	Ill Witch	81686058
623	The Thing That Hides in the Mud	1818076
624	High Tide Gyojin	54579801
625	Fairy of the Fountain	81563416
626	Amazon of the Seas	1796811
627	Nekogal #2	43352213
628	Witch's Apprentice	80741828
629	Armored Rat	16246527
630	Ancient Lizard Warrior	43230671
631	Maiden of the Moonlight	79629370
632	Stone Ogre Grotto	15023985
633	Winged Egg of New Life	42418084
634	Night Lizard	78402798
635	Queen's Double	05901497
636	Blue Winged Crown	41396436
637	Trent	78780140
638	Queen of the Autumn Leaves	04179849
639	Amphibious Bugroth	40173854
640	Acid Crawler	77568553
641	Invader of the Throne	03056267
642	Mystical Sheep #1	30451366
643	Disk Magician	76446915
644	Flame Viper	02830619
645	Royal Guard	39239728
646	Gruesome Goo	65623423
647	Hyosube	02118022
648	Machine Attacker	38116136
649	Hibikime	64501875
650	Whiptail Crow	91996584
651	Kunai with Chain	37390589
652	Magical Labyrinth	64389297
653	Warrior Elimination	90873992
654	Salamandra	32268901
655	Cursebraker	69666645

Number	Card	Password
656	Eternal Rest	95051344
657	Megamorph	22046459
658	Metalmorph	68540058
659	Winged Trumpeter	94939166
660	Stain Storm	21323861
661	Crush Card	57728570
662	Eradicading Aerosol	94716515
663	Breath of Light	20101223
664	Eternal Drought	56606928
665	Curse of the Millennium Shield	83094937
666	Yamadron Ritual	29089635
667	Gate Guardian Ritual	56483330
668	Bright Castle	82878489
669	Shadow Spell	29267084
670	Black Luster Ritual	55761792
671	Zera Ritual	81756897
672	Harpie's Feather Duster	18144506
673	War-Lion Ritual	54539105
674	Beastry Mirror Ritual	81933259
675	Ultimate Dragon	17928958
676	Commencement Dance	43417563
677	Hamburger Recipe	80811661
678	Revival of Sengenjin	16206366
679	Novox's Prayer	43694075
680	Curse of Tri-Horned Dragon	79699070
681	House of Adhesive Tape	15083728
682	Eatgaboon	42578427
683	Bear Trap	78977532
684	Invisible Wire	15361130
685	Acid Trap Hole	41356845
686	Widespread Ruin	77754944
687	Goblin Fan	04149689
688	Bad Reaction to Simochi	40633297
689	Reverse Trap	77622396
690	Fake Trap	03027001
691	Revival of Serpent Night Dragon	39411600
692	Turtle Oath	76806714
693	Contruct of Mask	02304453
694	Resurrection of Chakra	39399168
695	Puppet Ritual	05783166
696	Javelin Beetle Pact	41182875
697	Garma Sword Oath	78577570
698	Cosmo Queen's Prayer	04561679
699	Revival of Skeleton Rider	31066283

Number	Card	Password
700	Fortress Whale's Oath	77454922
701	Performance of Sword	04849037
702	Hungery Burger	30243636
703	Sengenjin	76232340
704	Skull Guardian	03627449
705	Tri-Horned Dragon	39111158
706	Serpent Night Dragon	66516792
707	Skull Knight	02504891
708	Cosmo Queen	38999506
709	Charka	65393205
710	Crab Turtle	91782219
711	Mikazukinoyaiba	38277918
712	Meteor Dragon	64271667
713	Meteor B. Dragon	90660762
714	Firewing Pegasus	27054370
715	Psyco Puppet	63459075
716	Garma Sword	90844184
717	Javelin Beetle	26932788
718	Fortress Whale	62337487
719	Dokurorider	99721536
720	Mask of Shine and Dark	25110231
721	Dark	76792184
722	Magician of Black Chaos	30208479

Games List

Xbox™

ATV QUAD POWER RACING 2

All Riders

Enter BUBBA as a profile name.

All Vehicles

Enter GENERALLEE as a profile name.

All Tracks

Enter ROADKILL as a profile name.

All Championships

Enter REDROOSTER as a profile name.

All Challenges

Enter DOUBLEBARREL as a profile name.

Maxed Out Skill Level

Enter FIDDLERSELBOW as a profile name.

Maxed Out Stats

Enter GINGHAM as a profile name.

BALDUR'S GATE: DARK ALLIANCE

All Spells

During gameplay, hold Y + A + L all the way + R halfway, then press the Left Thumbstick right.

Invincibility and Level Warp

During gameplay, hold Y + A + L all the way + R halfway + Left Thumbstick right, then press START.

BATMAN VENGEANCE

Master Code

At the Main menu press L, R, L, R, X, X, Y, Y.

Unlimited Electric Batarangs

At the Main menu press L, R, B, White, L.

Unlimited Batarangs

At the Main menu press L, R, White, Y.

BATTLE ENGINE AQUILA

Level Select

Start a new game and enter !EVAH!.

God Mode

Start a new game and enter B4K42.

All Bonuses

Start a new game and enter I05770Y2.

BIG MUTHA TRUCKERS

Select Cheats from the Options screen and enter the following:

All Cheats

Enter CHEATINGMUTHATRUCKER.

Level Select

Enter LAZYPLAYER.

Unlimited Time
Enter PUBLICTRANSPORT.

Diplomatic Immunity
Enter VICTORS.

$10 Million
Enter LOTSAMONEY.

Disable Damage
Enter 6WL.

Evil Truck
Enter VARLEY.

Automatic Sat Nav
Enter USETHEFORCE.

Fast Truck
Enter GINGERBEER.

Small Pedestrians
Enter DAISHI.

BLOODRAYNE

Cheat List

Select Enter Cheat from the Options screen and enter the following. Pause the game and choose Cheats to toggle the cheats on/off or activate them.

Code	Enter
Gratuitous Dismemberment	INSANEGIBSMODEGOOD
Enemies Thawed/Frozen	DONTFARTONOSCAR
God Mode	TRIASSASSINDONTDIE
Juggy Mode	JUGGYDANCESQUAD
Restore Health	LAMEYANKEEDONTFEED
Show Weapons On Body	SHOWMEMYWEAPONS

Level Select

Enter ONTHELEVEL as a cheat. Highlight New and press X + A to access the Level Select option.

Secret Louisiana Level

Enter BRIMSTONEINTHEBAYOU.

Messages

Enter the following cheats to view a message from the developers:

ACTIVE
ACTIVEACTIVEACTIVEACTIVE
ALBATROSS
ANGRYINSANEDUCK
BANANAFORTHEMONEY
COOLIGLOOFORME
COOLMAJESCO
COOLTRI
DANCEJUGGYDANCE
DANCETHETANGO
DASTARDLYFARTQUEEN
DELTAFOXTROTECHOTANGO
DIEMAJESCO
DIETRI
DOGEATDOG
DON'TCHEAT
DON'TDIE
EATDUCK
EATME
EATTHISPURPLEBANANA
FEEDONME
FEEDROMEOTHEDOG
FOXTROTUNIFORM-
CHARLEYKILO
GODHELPME
GODISGOOD
GODMODE
GOODGODHELPME
HIDETHEGIBS
HIDEWHISKEYATWORK
IAMADAM
IAMANGRY
IAMASSASSIN
IAMGOD
IAMINSANE
IAMJIMMY
IAMMAJESCO
IAMTRI
ICANDIE
ICHEAT

IEATDUCK
IEATSPAM
IHIDESPAM
IHUNTFORSPAM
INSANELAMAUVULAENIGMA
ISJIMMYINSANE
ISOLATETAINTEDLAMA
IWASMAJESCO
IWASTRI
IWORKFORMAJESCO
IWORKFORTRI
JIMMYRULES
JUGGYSHOWISKILLER
MANSHOW
MYDOGISPSYCHIC
MYKILOISLATE
MYKIMMYISUP
MYLAZYBANANA
MYUVULAISPURPLE
NAKEDMONSTER
NAKEDNASTYMONSTER
NOCHEATACTIVE
PAPADON'TPREACHER
PICKMYMONKEY
PSYCHICASSASSIN
QUEBECISCOOL
RAID
REALITYISTERMINAL
REALITYISTHECONUNDRUM
SCARLETCRANE
SHOWMEYOUMONKEY
SHOWMEYOURNASTY
SHOWMYNAKEDMONSTER
SPAMSPAMSPAMSPAM
STAINMYUNIFORM
TAKEMYWEAPONS
TERMINALREALITYISCOOL
TERMINALREALITYISLAME
TERMINALREALITYRULES

TERMINALSTAIN
TERMINALVELOCITY
THEMATRIX
THERULESAREOBSOLETE
THISISREALITY
UVULA
WEAPONSON

WHISKEYAL-
PHADELTAFOXTROT
YANKMYALPHABANANA
YOURFARTISDASTARDLY
YOURGODISCOOL

CHASE: HOLLYWOOD STUNT DRIVER

Select Career Mode and enter the following as the username:

Unlock Everything

Enter Dare Angel.

All Cars and Challenges

Enter Ride On.

All Cars and Multiplayer Modes

Enter BAM4FUN.

Level Select

Enter Action Star.

CONFLICT DESERT STORM

Cheat Mode

At the Main menu, press X, X, Y, Y, press Left Analog Stick (x2), Right Analog Stick (x2), press L, L, R, R. Pause the game to find the Cheats in the Options screen.

CRAZY TAXI 3: HIGH ROLLER

No Destination Mark and Arrow

At the Character Select screen, hold White + Black and press A. The word "Expert" appears at the bottom of the screen when entered correctly.

No Arrows

At the Character Select screen, hold White and press A. The message "no arrows" appears at the bottom of the screen when entered correctly.

No Destination Mark

At the Character Select screen, hold Black and press A. The message "no destination mark" appears at the bottom of the screen when entered correctly.

DEATHROW

Unlock Everything

Enter the name SOUTHEND.

All Teams and Players

Name Player 4 ALL150.

All Arenas

Name Player 4 MORE-ROOM.

Extreme Difficulty

Name Player 4 NO FEAR.

Multidisc

Name Player 4 CON-FUSED.

DR. MUTO

Select Cheats from the Options screen to enter the following:

Invincibility

Enter NECROSCI. This doesn't work when falling from high above.

Never Take Damage

Enter CHEATERBOY.

Unlock Every Gadget

Enter TINKERTOY.

Unlock Every Morph

Enter EUREKA.

Go Anywhere

Enter BEAMMEUP.

Secret Morphs

Enter LOGGLOGG.

See the Movies

Enter HOTTICKET.

Super Ending

Enter BUZZOFF.

DRAGON'S LAIR 3D

Cheat Mode

At the Main menu press R + Left Analog, R + Right Analog, R + Left Analog, R + Right Analog, R + White, R + Black, R + White, R + Black.

DYNASTY WARRIORS 3

All Shu Generals

At the Main menu, press White, Black, X, Y, White, R, L, Black.

BGM Test

At the Main menu, press L, White, Y, R, White, Black, X, Y.

Opening Edit

At the Main menu, press X, Black, Y, White, L, R, White, White.

Bonus Movies

At the Opening Edit screen, highlight Replay, hold L + R and press A. Hold Black + White and press A for another bonus movie.

ENTER THE MATRIX

Cheat Mode

After playing through the hacking system and unlocking CHEAT.EXE, use CHEAT.EXE to enter the following:

Effect	Code
All Guns	0034AFFF
Infinite Ammo	1DDF2556
Invisibility	FFFFFFF1
Infinite Focus	69E5D9E4
Infinite Health	7F4DF451
Speedy Logos	7867F443
Unlock Secret Level	13D2C77F
Fast Focus Restore	FFF0020A
Test Level	13D2C77F
Enemies Can't Hear You	4516DF45
Turbo Mode	FF00001A
Multiplayer Fight	D5C55D1E
Low Gravity	BB013FFF
Taxi Driving	312MF451

GHOST RECON

After completing all of the objectives, you can enter the following cheats. During gameplay, press Back and enter the following:

Team Invincibility

Press B, A, Y, Y, A, B, X (x3).

Big Heads

Press A, X, B, Y, A.

Paper Mode

Press B, A, X, Y, A.

Chicken Explosives

Press X, X, Y, A, B.

High-Pitched Voices

Press X, A, Y, B, X.

Slow Motion

Press Y, Y, B, X, A.

GODZILLA: DESTROY ALL MONSTERS MELEE

At the Main menu, press and hold L, B, R, then release B, R, L (*in that order*). Enter the following codes:

Code	Enter
Twelve Continues in Adventure	548319
All Gallery	962129

All Cities and Monsters	863768
All Monsters, Except Orga	753079
All Monsters	209697

Godzilla 2000	637522
Rodan	724284
Destoroyah	352117
Gigan	822777
King Ghidorah	939376
Mecha-Ghidorah	504330
Mecha Godzilla 2	643861
Orga	622600

All Cities	107504
Monster Island Level	745749
Mothership Level	972094
Boxing Ring Level	440499

Military	728629
Energy Doesn't Recharge, More Damage	690242

Player Indicators Visible	860068
No HUD	880460
Hedorah	288730
No Hedorah	584408
Add AI Player to Melee	154974
P1 Is Small	558277
P2 Is Small	689490
P3 Is Small	203783
P4 Is Small	495355
Even Players Are Small	600095
Odd Players Are Small	853955
All Players Are Small	154974

Player Regenerates Health	597378
P1 Invincible	152446
P2 Invincible	724689
P3 Invincible	367744
P4 Invincible	317320
All Invincible	569428
P1 Deals 4x Damage	940478
P2 Deals 4x Damage	930041
P3 Deals 4x Damage	537651
P4 Deals 4x Damage	889610
All Deal 4x Damage	817683
Military Deals 4x Damage	970432
Throw All Buildings and Objects	248165
Indestructible Buildings	451129
P1 Invisible	659672
P2 Invisible	493946
All Monsters Invisible	600225
P1 Full Energy	778393

P2 Full Energy	881557
P3 Full Energy	597558
P4 Full Energy	218967
No Freeze Tanks	223501
No Power-ups	229497
No Health Power-ups	221086
No Energy Power-ups	803358
No Mothra Power-ups	491040
No Rage Power-ups	666500
Only Energy Power-ups	553945
Only Rage Power-ups	660398
Only Health Power-Ups	270426
P1 Always in Rage	159120
P2 Always in Rage	491089
P3 Always in Rage	450514
P4 Always in Rage	702905
Black-and-White	860475
Technicolor	394804
Game Version (in options)	097401

Credits	339223

GRAVITY GAMES BIKE: STREET. VERT. DIRT.

Select Cheat Code from the Options screen and enter the following:

Unlock Everything
Enter LOTACRAP.

All Bikes
Enter PIKARIDE.

Angus Sigmund
Enter SIGMAN.

Bird Brains
Enter FLYAWAY.

Bobby Bones
Enter BONEGUY.

Pierce
Enter BADGIRL.

Ramp Granny
Enter OLDLADY.

Max Stats
Enter MAXSTATS.

Dennis McCoy Max Stats
Enter DMCDMAN.

Oil Refinery
Enter OILSPILL.

Train Depot
Enter CHOOCHOO.

Museum District
Enter ARTRIDER.

Museum District Competition
Enter ARTCOMP.

Fuzzy's Yard
Enter FUZYDIRT.

Mount Magma
Enter VOLCANO.

Gravity Games Street
Enter PAVEMENT.

Gravity Games Vert
Enter GGFLYER.

Gravity Games Dirt
Enter MUDPUDLE.

Andre Ellison's Movie
Enter ANDFMV.

Dennis McCoy's Movie
Enter DMCFMV.

Fuzzy Hall's Movie
Enter FUZFMV.

Jamie Bestwick's Movie
Enter JAMFMV.

Leigh Ramsdell's Movie
Enter LEIFMV.

Mat Berringer's Movie
Enter MATFMV.

Reuel Erikson's Movie
Enter REUFMV.

HITMAN 2: SILENT ASSASSIN

Level Select
At the Main menu, press R, L, Up, Down, Y, B.

Complete Level
During gameplay, press R, L, Up, Down, A, X, press Left Analog Stick, B, A, B, A.

All Weapons
During gameplay, press R, L, Up, Down, A, Up, X, A.

Invincibilty
During gameplay, press R, L, Up, Down, A, R, L, Black, White.

Full Heal
During gameplay, press R, L, Up, Down, A, Up, Down.

Toggle Lethal Charge
During gameplay, press L, R, Up, Down, A, Black, Black.

Gravity
During gameplay, press R, L, Up, Down, A, L, L.

Slow Motion
During gameplay, press R, L, Up, Down, A, Up, L.

Megaforce
During gameplay, press R, L, Up, Down, A, R, R.

Toggle Bomb Mode
During gameplay, press R, L, Up, Down, A, Up, White.

Toggle Punch Mode
During gameplay, press R, L, Up, Down, A, Up, Up.

Toggle Nailgun Mode
During gameplay, press R, L, Up, Down A, White, White.

JAMES BOND 007: NIGHTFIRE

Select Codenames from the Main menu and choose a codename. Then pick Secret Unlocks to enter the following codes. Save your codename before exiting this menu.

Level Select
Enter PASSPORT.

Alpine Escape Level
Enter POWDER.

Enemies Vanquished Level
Enter TRACTION.

Double Cross Level
Enter BONSAI.

Night Shift Level
Enter HIGHRISE.

Chain Reaction Level
Enter MELTDOWN.

Phoenix Fire Level
Enter FLAME.

Deep Descent Level
Enter AQUA.

Island Infiltration Level
Enter PARADISE.

Decrypter Upgrade
Enter SESAME.

Countdown Level
Enter BLASTOFF.

Equinox Level
Enter VACUUM.

All Gadget Upgrades
Enter Q LAB.

Camera Upgrade
Enter SHUTTER.

Grapple Upgrade
Enter LIFTOFF.

Laser Upgrade
Enter PHOTON.

Scope Upgrade
Enter SCOPE.

Stunner Upgrade
Enter ZAP.

Tranquilizer Dart Upgrade
Enter SLEEPY.

Bigger Clip for Sniper Rifle
Enter MAGAZINE.

P2K Upgrade
Enter P2000.

Golden Wolfram P2K
Enter AU P2K.

Golden PP7
Enter AU PP7.

Vanquish Car Missile Upgrade
Enter LAUNCH.

All Multiplayer Scenarios
Enter GAMEROOM.

Uplink Multiplayer Scenario
Enter TRANSMIT.

Demolition Multiplayer Scenario
Enter TNT.

Protection Multiplayer Scenario
Enter GUARDIAN.

GoldenEye Strike Multiplayer Scenario
Enter ORBIT.

Assassination Multiplayer Scenario
Enter TARGET.

Team King of the Hill Multiplayer Scenario
Enter TEAMWORK.

Explosive Scenery Option, Multiplayer
Enter BOOM. Find this option in the Enviro-Mods menu.

All Characters, Multiplayer
Enter PARTY.

Play as Bond Tux, Multiplayer
Enter BLACKTIE.

Play as Drake Suit, Multiplayer
Enter NUMBER 1.

Play as Bond Spacesuit, Multiplayer
Enter ZERO G.

Play as Goldfinger, Multiplayer
Enter MIDAS.

Play as Renard, Multiplayer
Enter HEADCASE.

Play as Scaramanga, Multiplayer
Enter ASSASSIN.

Play as Christmas Jones, Multiplayer
Enter NUCLEAR.

Play as Nick Nack, Multiplayer
Enter BITESIZE.

Play as Max Zorin, Multiplayer
Enter BLIMP.

Play as Wai Lin, Multiplayer
Enter MARTIAL.

Play as Xenia Onatopp, Multiplayer
Enter JANUS.

Play as May Day, Multiplayer
Enter BADGIRL.

Play as Elektra King, Multiplayer
Enter SLICK.

Play as Jaws, Multiplayer
Enter DENTAL.

Play as Baron Samedi, Multiplayer
Enter VOODOO.

Play as Oddjob, Multiplayer
Enter BOWLER.

Play as Nick Nack, Multiplayer
Enter BITESIZE.

Play as Max Zorin, Multiplayer
Enter BLIMP.

Drive an SUV, Enemies Vanquished Level

Start the Enemies Vanquished Level and pause the game. Hold L and press X, B, Y, X, Y, then release L.

Race the Cobra, Enemies Vanquished Level

Start the Enemies Vanquished Level and pause the game. Hold L and press B, B, X, X, Y, then release L.

Enter the following codes during the Paris Prelude, Enemies Vanquished, Island Infiltration, or Deep Descent levels:

Faster Racing

Pause the game, hold L and press X, Y, B, Y, X, then release L.

Berserk Racing

Pause the game, hold L and press X, Y, Y, X, Y, B, then release L.

Trails

Pause the game, hold L and press X, B, B, X, then release L.

Double Armor

Pause the game, hold L and press B, Y, X, B, B, then release L.

Triple Armor

Pause the game, hold L and press B, Y, X, B, B, B, then release L.

Quadruple Armor

Pause the game, hold L and press B, Y, X, B (x4), then release L.

Super Bullets

Pause the game, hold L and press B (x4), release L.

JURASSIC PARK: OPERATION GENESIS

Gimme Some Money

During gameplay, press L + Up, L + Down, L + Up. This gives you $10,000.

Gimme Lots of Money

During gameplay, press L, Right, Right, L, R, Down. This gives you $250,000.

Where's the Money?

During gameplay, press L, R, L, R, Down, Down. This takes away all your money.

Impossible Mission

During gameplay, press R, Right (x4), R. This completes all of the missions.

All Research

During gameplay, press Down (x3), Left, Right, L, Down, Up.

Mr. DNA

During gameplay, press R, Up, R, Right, L, Down.

Rampage Time

During gameplay, press L, L, L, Left, Left, Left. This makes all carnivores rampage.

Extinction Event

During gameplay, press L, R, Down, R, L. This kills all dinosaurs.

Oh No!

During gameplay, press Left, Right, Left, Right, R. This kills all visitors.

Dial-A-Twister

During gameplay, press Left, Up, Right, Down, L + R.

No Twisters

During gameplay, press Left, Right, L, R, Left, Right, L, R.

Hot One

During gameplay, press R + Down, R + Down. This causes a heat wave.

Welcome to Melbourne

During gameplay, press R, R, L, R, Down, Up, Down. This causes it to rain.

Guaranteed Immunity

During gameplay, hold L + R and press Up, Up. Dinosaurs won't get sick.

No Red Tape

During gameplay, press L, R, Left, Down (x4). You aren't charged for deaths.

Open to the Public

During gameplay, press Left, Down, Right, Up, L + R, L + R. This gives you the selection of dig sites without the required stars.

Market Day

During gameplay, press Down, L, R, Down.

Sequencing Error

During gameplay, press Down, Up + R, L, Down. This gives 55% dinosaur genomes.

Drive-by

During gameplay, press R + L, Left, Down, Right, Right. The safari ride camera acts like a gun.

Crash!

During gameplay, hold R + L and press Up, Down, Up, Down.

Isla Muerta

During gameplay, press R, R, R, L, Right. Dinosaurs appear decayed.

MEDAL OF HONOR: FRONTLINE

Select Passwords from the Options menu and enter the following codes. You need to turn on many of these cheats at the Bonus screen.

Master Code
Enter ENCHILADA.

Mission Complete with Gold Star
Enter SALMON.

Mission 2: A Storm in the Port
Enter BASS.

Mission 3: Needle in a Haystack
Enter STURGEON.

Mission 4: Several Bridges Too Far
Enter PIKE.

Mission 5: Rolling Thunder
Enter TROUT.

Mission 6: The Horten's Nest
Enter CATFISH.

Silver Bullet Mode
Enter KILLSHOT.

Perfectionist
Enter ONESHOTGUN.

Achilles' Head
Enter CRANIUM.

Bullet Shield
Enter NOHITSFORU.

Snipe-O-Rama
Enter LONGVIEW.

Rubber Grenade
Enter FLUBBER.

Mohton Torpedoes
Enter TOPFUN.

Invisible Enemies
Enter GHOSTARMY.

Men with Hats
Enter BOOTDAHEAD.

A Good Day to "Dye" Video
Enter COTOBREATH.

From the Animator's Desk Video
Enter FLIPBOOK.

Making of D-Day FMV
Enter BACKSTAGEO.

Making of Storm in the Port FMV
Enter BACKSTAGET.

Making of Needle in a Hay Stack FMV
Enter BACKSTAGER.

Making of Several Bridges Too Far FMV
Enter BACKSTAGEF.

Making of Rolling Thunder FMV
Enter BACKSTAGEI.

Making of the Horten's Nest FMV
Enter BACKSTAGES.

MINORITY REPORT

Select Cheats from the Special menu and enter the following:

Invincibility
Enter LRGARMS.

Level Warp All
Enter PASSKEY.

Level Skip
Enter QUITER.

All Combos
Enter NINJA.

All Weapons
Enter STRAPPED.

Infinite Ammo
Enter MRJUAREZ.

Super Damage
Enter SPINACH.

Health
Enter BUTTERUP.

Select Alternate Heroes from the Special menu to find the following cheats:

Clown Hero
Enter SCARYCLOWN.

Convict Hero
Enter JAILBREAK.

GI John Hero
Enter GNRLINFANTRY.

Lizard Hero
Enter HISSSS.

Moseley Hero
Enter HAIRLOSS.

Nara Hero
Enter WEIGHTGAIN.

Nikki Hero
Enter BIGLIPS.

Robot Hero
Enter MRROBOTO.

Super John Hero
Enter SUPERJOHN.

Zombie Hero
Enter IAMSODEAD.

Free Aim
Enter FPSSTYLE.

Pain Arenas
Enter MAXIMUMHURT.

Armor
Enter STEELUP.

Baseball Bat
Enter SLUGGER.

Rag Doll
Enter CLUMSY.

Slo-Mo Button
Enter SLIZOMIZO.

Bouncy Men
Enter BOUNZMEN.

Wreck the Joint
Enter CLUTZ.

Dramatic Finish
Enter STYLIN.

Ending
Enter WIMP.

Concept Art
Enter SKETCHPAD.

All Movies

Enter DIRECTOR.

Do Not Select

Enter DONOTSEL.

MLB SLUGFEST 2004

Cheats

At the Match-Up screen, use X, Y and B to enter the following codes, then press the appropriate direction. For example, for "No Contact Mode" (433 Left) press X four times, Y three times, B three times, then press Left.

Code	Enter
Cheats Disabled	111 Down
Unlimited Turbo	444 Down
No Fatigue	343 Up
No Contact Mode	433 Left
16" Softball	242 Down
Rubber Ball	242 Up
Whiffle Bat	004 Right
Blade Bat	002 Up

Bone Bat	001 Up
Ice Bat	003 Up
Log Bat	004 Up
Mace Bat	004 Left

Spike Bat	005 Up
Big Head	200 Right
Tiny Head	200 Left
Max Batting	300 Left
Max Power	030 Left
Max Speed	003 Left
Alien Team	231 Down
Bobble Head Team	133 Down

Casey Team	233 Down
Dolphin Team	102 Down
Dwarf Team	103 Down
Eagle Team	212 Right
Evil Clown Team	211 Down

Gladiator Team	113 Down
Horse Team	211 Right
Lion Team	220 Right
Little League	101 Down
Minotaur Team	110 Down
Napalitano Team	232 Down

Olshan Team	222 Down
Pinto Team	210 Right
Rivera Team	222 Up
Rodeo Clown	132 Down
Scorpion Team	112 Down
Team Terry Fitzgerald	333 Right
Team Todd McFarlane	222 Right
Atlantis Stadium	321 Left
Coliseum Stadium	333 Up
Empire Park Stadium	321 Right
Forbidden City Stadium	333 Left
Midway Park Stadium	321 Down
Monument Stadium	333 Down
Rocket Park Stadium	321 Up

Extended Time for Codes	303 Up

MVP BASEBALL 2003

After creating the following players, make sure you sign and activate them.

Broken Bats

Create a player named Keegn Patersn, Jacob Patersn, or Ziggy Patersn.

Home Run Hitter

Create a player named Erik Kiss.

NBA 2K3

Codes

Select Game Play from the Options menu, hold Left on the D-pad + Right on the Left Thumbstick, then press START. Exit to the Options screen and a Codes option will appear.

Sega Sports, Visual Concepts and NBA 2K3 Teams

Enter MEGASTARS as a code.

Street Trash

Enter SPRINGER as a code.

Duotone Draw

Enter DUOTONE as a code.

NBA INSIDE DRIVE 2003

Select Codes from the Options screen and enter the following. Re-enter a code to disable it.

Unlimited Turbo
Enter SPEEDY.

Created Players All Points Available
Enter MOMONEY.

Easy Three-Pointers
Enter THREE4ALL.

Easy Alley Oops
Enter DUNKONYOU.

Tiny Players
Enter ITSYBITSY.

8-Ball
Enter CORNERPOCKET.

ABA Ball
Enter STYLIN70S.

Beach Ball
Enter BEACHBUMS.

Soccer Ball
Enter KICKME.

Volleyball
Enter SPIKEIT.

WNBA Ball
Enter GOTGAME.

Xbox Ball
Enter XBALL.

Chicago Skyline Stadium (Single Game)
Enter CITYHOOPS.

Accept All Trades
Enter DOIT.

Allow Hidden Players
Enter PEEKABOO. Create a player with the following names for classic versions of each:

Patrick Ewing

Shawn Kemp

Michael Jordan

Karl Malone

Reggie Miller

Hakeem Olajuwon

Scottie Pippen

NBA LIVE 2003

Select Roster Management from the Team Management menu, then create a player with the following last names. These characters will be available as free agents.

B-Rich

Enter DOLLABILLS.

Busta Rhymes

Enter FLIPMODE.

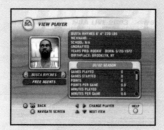

DJ Clue

Enter MIXTAPES.

Fabolous

Enter GHETTOFAB.

Hot Karl

Enter CALIFORNIA.

Just Blaze

Enter GOODBEATS.

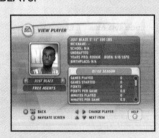

NBA STARTING FIVE

Big Heads

Enter BIGHEAD.

Big Feet

Enter BIGFOOT.

Big Hands

Enter BIGHAND.

Flat Players

Enter PANCAKE.

First Pick in Draft

Enter FIRSTPICK.

Red, White, and Blue Hats

Enter SILKHAT.

Glasses with Nose and Mustache

Enter PARTYGLASSES.

NBA STREET VOL. 2

Select Pick Up Game, hold L and enter the following codes when "Enter cheat codes now" appears at the bottom of the screen:

Unlimited Turbo
  Press X, X, Y, Y.

ABA Ball
  Press B, X, B, X.

WNBA Ball
  Press B, Y, Y, B.

No Display Bars
  Press X, B (x3).

All Jerseys
  Press B, Y, X, X.

All Courts

Press X, Y, Y, X.

St. Lunatics Team and All Street Legends

Press X, Y, B, Y.

All NBA Legends

Press B, Y, Y, X.

Classic Michael Jordan

Press B, Y, B, B.

Explosive Rims

Press B (x3), Y.

Small Players

Press Y, Y, B, X.

Big Heads

Press B, X, X, B.

No Counters

Press Y, Y, B, B.

Ball Trails

Press Y, Y, Y, X.

All Quicks

Press Y, B, Y, X.

Easy Shots

Press Y, B, X, Y.

Hard Shots

Press Y, X, B, Y.

NFL FEVER 2003

Select User Profile and create a user profile with the following names:

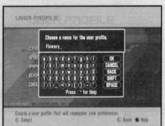

Stadiums

Stadium	Enter
Commandos	Barracks

Pansies	Flowery
Pyramid	Sphinx
Samurai	Warrior

Tumbleweeds	Dustball

Teams

Team	Enter
1964 Browns	Bigrun
1967 Packers	Cheese
1972 Dolphins	Perfect
1977 Cowboys	Thehat
1978 Steelers	Curtain
1983 Raiders	Outlaws
1985 Bears	Sausage
1989 49ers	Empire
1993 Cowboys	Lonestar
1996 Packers	Green

1998 Broncos	Milehigh
Chromides	Regulate

Commandos	Camo
Cows	Milk
Creampuffs	Cakewalk
Crocs	Crykie
DaRulas	Tut
Eruption	Lava
Firemen	Blazer
Gladiators	BigBack
Hackers	Axemen
King Cobras	Venom
Mimes	Silence
Monks	Robes

Pansies	Viola
Polars	Igloo
Samurai	Slasher
Skeletons	Stone
Soldiers	Helmet
Sorcerers	Spellboy

Spies	Target
Thunder Sheep	Flock
Tumbleweeds	Dusty
War Elephants	Horns
Wildcats	Kitty
Winged Gorillas	Flying

NICKELODEON PARTY BLAST

Secret Characters

Select Blast and press Down, Down, Right, Left, Right, Up, Left, Down, Right.

Clam Games

Select Blast and press Up, Up, Down, Down, Left, Right.

Bungi Games

At the Game Select screen, highlight Bungi and press Up, Up, Down, Down, Left, Right.

PRO RACE DRIVER

Enter the following codes at the Bonus screen:

Realistic Handling

Enter SIM.

Enhanced Damage

Enter DAMAGE.

Credits

Enter CREDITS.

QUANTUM REDSHIFT

Enter CHEAT as your name, then enter the following codes:

All Characters

Enter Nematode.

All Speeds

Enter zoomZOOM.

Upgrade All Ships

Enter RICEitup.

Unlimited Turbo

Enter FishFace.

Infinite Shields

Enter ThinkBat.

RED FACTION II

Select Cheats from the Extras menu and enter the following codes:

Unlock Everything

Press White, White, X, X, Y, Black, Y, Black.

All Cheats

Press Y, Black, White, Black, Y, X, White, X.

Level Select

Press Black, Y, X, White, Y, Black, X, X.

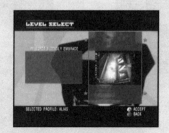

Super Health

Press X, X, Y, White, Y, White, Black.

Infinite Grenades

Press Black, X, Black, Y, X, Black, X, Black.

Director's Cut

Press Y, X, Black, White, Black, X, Y, White.

Rapid Rails

Press Black, Y, Black, Y, X, X, White, White.

Extra Chunky

Press Black (x4), White, X, Black, Black.

Infinite Ammo

Press Y, White, X, Black, Y, Black, X, White.

Wacky Deaths

Press White (x8).

Walking Dead

Press X (x8).

Rain of Fire Cheat

Press Y (x8).

Gibby Explosions

Press White, Black, X, Y, White, Black, X, Y.

Explosive Personality

Press X.

REDCARD SOCCER 2003

All Teams, Stadiums, and Finals Mode

Enter BIGTANK as a profile name.

ROCKY

Punch Double Damage

At the Main menu, hold R and press Right, Down, Left, Up, Left, L.

Double Speed Boxing

At the Main menu, hold R and press Down, Left, Down, Up, Right, L.

All Default Boxers and Arenas

At the Main menu, hold R and press Right, Down, Up, Left, Up, L. This *doesn't* unlock Mickey or the Rocky Statue.

All Default Boxers, Arenas, and Rocky Statue

At the Main menu, hold R and press Right (x3), Left, Right, L.

All Default Boxers, Arenas, Rocky Statue, and Mickey

At the Main menu, hold R and press Up, Down, Down, Left, Left, L.

Full Stats, Tournament and Exhibition Modes

At the Main menu, hold R and press Left, Up, Up, Down, Right, L.

Full Stats, Movie Mode

At the Main menu, hold R and press Right, Down, Down, Up, Left, L.

Win Fight, Movie Mode

At the Main menu, hold R and press Right, Right, Left, Left, Up, L. During a fight, press Black + White to win.

ROLLER COASTER TYCOON

Select a guest and change his/her name to one of the following:

Photographer

Enter Chris Sawyer.

Artist

Enter Simon Foster.

Waving

Enter Katie Brayshaw.

"Wow!"

Enter John Wardley.

SERIOUS SAM

Cheats

At the Main menu, click and hold the Left Thumbstick and press Black, White, Y.

SPLINTER CELL

Level Select

Enter !LAMAUDITE! as a Profile Name.

STAR WARS JEDI KNIGHT II: JEDI OUTCAST

Select Cheats from the Extras menu to enter the following codes:

Invulnerable

Enter BUBBLE.

Inifinite Ammo

Enter BISCUIT.

All Characters in Jedi Arena

Enter PEEPS.

Start with Lightsaber
Enter FUDGE.

All FMVs
Enter FLICKY.

Level Select
Enter CHERRY.

STAR WARS: JEDI STARFIGHTER

Select Codes from the Options screen to enter the following:

Unlock Everything
Enter LONGO.

Headhunter Ship
Enter HUNTER.

Invincible

Enter ARTOO.

No HUD

Enter CONVISTA.

Jar Jar Mode

Enter JARJAR.

Director Mode

Enter DARON.

STAR WARS: THE CLONE WARS

Select Bonuses from the Options menu, then select Codes to enter the following:

Unlimited Ammo

Enter NOHONOR.

All Multiplayer Maps

Enter LETSDANCE.

Team Photos

Enter YOURMASTERS.

All Cutscenes

Enter GOTPOPCORN.

Three Bonus Objectives
Enter ALITTLEHELP.

All Bonus Menu Items
Enter IGIVEUP.

STATE OF EMERGENCY

Invulnerable
During gameplay, press White, L, Black, R, A.

Unlimited Ammo
During gameplay, press White, L, Black, R, Y.

Complete Current Mission

During gameplay, press Left (x4), Y.

Infinite Time in Chaos Mode

During gameplay, press White, L, Black, R, B.

Little Player

During gameplay, press Black, R, White, L, A.

Big Player

During gameplay, press Black, R, White, L, Y.

Normal Player

During gameplay, press Black, R, White, L, B.

Punches Decapitate

During gameplay, press White, L, Black, R, X.

Looting on the Rise

During gameplay, press Black, White, R, L, Y.

Bull

During gameplay, press Right (x4), A.

Freak

During gameplay, press Right (x4), B.

Spanky

During gameplay, press Right (x4), Y.

AK-47
During gameplay, press Left, Right, Down, R, Y.

Flamethrower
During gameplay, press Left, Right, Down, Black, B.

Grenade
During gameplay, press Left, Right, Down, R, X.

Grenade Launcher
During gameplay, press Left, Right, Down, Black, X.

M-16
During gameplay, press Left, Right, Down, R, B.

Minigun
During gameplay, press Left, Right, Down, Black, Y.

Molotov Cocktail
During gameplay, press Left, Right, Down, R, A.

Pepper Spray
During gameplay, press Left, Right, Down, White, X.

Pistol
During gameplay, press Left, Right, Down, White, Y.

Rocket Launcher
During gameplay, press Left, Right, Down, Black, A.

Shotgun

During gameplay, press Left, Right, Down, L, Y.

Tazer

During gameplay, press Left, Right, Down, White, B.

Tear Gas

During gameplay, press Left, Right, Down, White, A.

STEEL BATTALION

All VTs and Levels in Free Mission Mode

At the Title screen, use the tuner and point it at the following numbers (in order) for one second each:

1, 9, 7, 9, 0, 9, 0, 6

STREET HOOPS

Select Cheats from the Game Settings option to enter the following:

Brick City Clothing

Press R, Black, R, L, Y, X, R, L.

Clown Uniform

Press X, L, X, Y.

Cowboy Uniform

Press Y, White, White, R.

Elvis Uniforms

Press Y, Black, White, Black, Black, White, L, Black.

Kung Fu Uniform

Press Y, Y, X, L.

Pimp Uniforms
Press R, X, Y, Black.

Santa Uniform
Press White, Black, White, Black.

Tuxedo Uniform
Press Black, Black, Y, X.

Normal Ball
Press R, X, X, L.

ABA Ball
Press Y, White, X, White.

Court Select Ball
Press Y, X, Y, L, Y, X, X.

Black Ball
Press White, White, Y, Black.

Theft Mode (Easier Steals)
Press R, X (x3), R, Black, Y, White.

Block Party (Easier Blocks)
Press R, Y, Black, White.

Power Game
Press White, Y, Black, Y.

Fast Clock
Press Y, Y, Y, X, X, X, L, Black.

Perfect Field Goals
Press Y, Y, Y, X, X, X, R, White.

SUPERMAN: THE MAN OF STEEL

All Levels and Bonuses
Pause the game and press R, Black, Y, Black, L, White.

Unlimited Health
Pause the game and press Black, White, L, X, L, White.

X-Ray Graphics

Pause the game and press L, L, R, L, Y, X, White, Black, Black, White.

Freeze Graphics

Pause the game and press R, L, Black, White, L, Y, Y, Black, R, White.

THE ELDER SCROLLS III: MORROWIND

During gameplay, access the Options screen. Go to the Statistics page to enter the following codes. You can only enter one code at a time.

Restore Health

Highlight Health and press Black, White, Black (x3). Hold A until you reach a desired level.

Restore Magicka

Highlight Magicka and press Black, White, White, Black, White. Hold A until you reach a desired level.

Restore Fatigue

Highlight Fatigue and press Black, Black, White, White, Black. Hold A until you reach a desired level.

THE LORD OF THE RINGS: THE TWO TOWERS

Health

Pause the game, hold L + R and press Y, Down, A, Up.

Arrows

Pause the game, hold L + R and press A, Down, Y, Up.

1000 Upgrade Points

Pause the game, hold L + R and press A, Down (x3).

Level 2 Skills

Pause the game, hold L + R and press B, Right, B, Right.

Level 4 Skills

Pause the game, hold L + R and press Y, Up, Y, Up.

Level 6 Skills

Pause the game, hold L + R and press X, Left, X, Left.

Level 8 Skills

Pause the game, hold L + R and press A, A, Down, Down.

You must first complete the game to enter the following codes:

Always Devastating

Pause the game, hold L + R and press X, X, B, B.

Small Enemies

Pause the game, hold L + R and press Y, Y, A, A.

All Upgrades

Pause the game, hold L + R and press Y, B, Y, B.

Invulnerable

Pause the game, hold L + R and press Y, X, A, B.

Slow Motion

Pause the game, hold L + R and press Y, B, A, X.

Unlimited Missile Weapons

Pause the game, hold L + R and press X, B, A, Y.

THE SIMS

At the Main menu, press L + R, then enter the following codes:

Play The Sims Mode, All 2-Player Games, Objects, and Skins

Enter MIDAS. Select Get A Life and start a new game. Join Roxy in the hot tub, pause the game, and quit.

The Party Motel 2-Player Game

Enter PARTY M.

First-Person View

Enter FISH EYE. Press B to toggle the view.

TIGER WOODS PGA TOUR 2003

Select Cheat Codes from the Options screen to enter the following codes:

All Golfers and Courses

Enter ALLTW3.

All Golfers (except Josey Scott)

Enter ALL28G.

All Courses

Enter 14COURSES.

Super Tiger Woods
Enter SUNDAY.

Cedric "Ace" Andrews
Enter IAM#1.

Stuart Appleby
Enter ORANGES.

Notah Begay III
Enter NOTABLY.

Mark Calavecchia
Enter CALCULATE.

Stewart Cink
Enter SINK.

Dominic "The Don" Donatello
Enter GODFATHER.

Brad Faxon
Enter XON.

Jim Furyk
Enter THESWING.

Charles Howell III
Enter BANDPANTS.

Justin Leonard
Enter JUSTINTIME.

Solita Lopez
Enter SOLITARY1.

Hamish "Mulligan" McGregor
Enter MCRUFF.

Takeharu "Tsunami" Moto
Enter 2TON.

Kellie Newman
Enter COWGIRL.

Mark O'Meara
Enter TB.

Vijay Singh
Enter VJSING.

Steve Stricker
Enter SS.

Val "Sunshine" Summers
Enter VALENTINE.

Melvin "Yosh" Tanigawa
Enter YOYOYO.

Ty Tryon
Enter TYNO.

Josey "Superstar" Scott
Enter SUPERSTAR.

TONY HAWK'S PRO SKATER 4

Select Cheat Codes from the Options screen to enter the following codes:

Unlock Everything

Enter watch_me_xplode. You must turn on the cheats by selecting Cheats from the Options screen during gameplay.

Daisy

Enter (o)(o).

Always Special

Enter i'myellow.

Perfect Rail

Enter belikeeric.

Perfect Skitch

Enter bumperrub.

Stats 13

Enter 4p0sers.

Perfect Manual

Enter freewheelie.

Moon Gravity

Enter moon$hot.

Matrix Mode

Enter fbiagent.

Secret Created Skaters

Enter the following names for hidden created skaters:

#$%@!

Aaron Skillman

Adam Lippmann

Andrew Skates

Andy Marchal

Angus

Atiba Jefferson

Ben Scott Pye

Big Tex

Brian Jennings	DDT
Captain Liberty	DeadEndRoad
Chauwa Steel	Fritz
Chris Peacock	Gary Jesdanun
ConMan	grjost
Danaconda	Henry Ji
Dave Stohl	

Jason Uyeda	Kenzo
Jim Jagger	Kevin Mulhall
Joe Favazza	Kraken
John Rosser	Lindsey Hayes
Jow	Lisa G Davies

Little Man

Marilena Rixfor

Mat Hoffman

Matt Mcpherson

Maya's Daddy

Meek West

Mike Day

Mike Lashever

Mike Ward

Mr. Brad

Nolan Nelson

Parking Guy

Peasus

Pete Day

Pooper

Rick Thorne

Sik

Stacey D

Zac ZiG Drake

Stacey Ytuarte

Team Chicken

Ted Barber

Todd Wahoske

Top Bloke

Wardcore

TOTAL IMMERSION RACING

Enter the following as a career name:

All Cars

Enter Loaded.

CART Car
Enter Downforce.

Low Gravity
Enter Feather.

All Tracks
Enter Road Sweeps.

Slow Motion
Enter Poke.

Extreme Difficulty
Enter Road Trip.

Disable HUD
Enter No Dogs.

Slow CPU Cars
Enter Walk It.

WAKEBOARDING UNLEASHED

At the Main menu, enter the following codes. You should get the corresponding message when the code is entered correctly.

Boards 2 and 3
Message: YOU GOT ALL THE BOARDS… OR DID YOU?

Press Up, Up, Left, Left, Right, Right, Down, Down, Up, Left, Right, Down, Up, Left, Right, Down.

All Levels
Message: TRAVEL VISA APPROVED

Press X (x4), A (x4), Y (x4), X, A, Y.

100% of Everything
Message: ULTIMATE CHEAT…

Press Up, Down, Up, Down, Up, Down, Up, Down, Up, Down, Left, Right, Left, Right, Left, Right, Left, Right, Left, Right.

WHACKED!

Enter the following as a profile name in Gameshow mode:

Uber Mode
Enter UBERHUNGARIAN.

All Arenas, Weapons, Weapon Sets, and FMVs
Enter AROUNDDAWORLD.

All Weapons and FMVs
Enter TIMEFORCHAOS.

All Characters, Food Products, Burgers, and FMVs
Enter FOODFIGHT.

All Characters and FMVs
Enter DOUBLEDOUBLE.

WHITEOUT

All Tracks, Characters, and Snowmobiles
At the Main menu, hold L + R and press Right (x4).

All Tracks
At the Main menu, hold L + R and press Up (x4).

All Characters
At the Main menu, hold L + R and press Down (x4).

All Parts
At the Main menu, hold L + R and press Left (x4).

X2: WOLVERINE'S REVENGE

Unlock Everything
At the Main menu, press X, L, X, L, X, X, L, R, X, L, X, L, X, X, L, R.

Level Select & All Challenges
At the Main menu, press X, L, X, L, X, L, L, R.

All Cerebro Files and Movies

At the Main menu, press X, L, X, L, X, X, R, L.

All Costumes

At the Main menu, press X, L, X, L, X, X, L, R.

Cheats

At the Main menu, press X, X, L (x4), X, X, L. Pause the game to find the Cheats.

X-MEN: NEXT DIMENSION

Unlock All

At the Main menu, hold L and press Right, Right, Left, Left, Down, Up, B.

Games List

ATV QUAD POWER RACING 2

All Riders

Enter BUBBA as a profile name.

All Vehicles

Enter GENERALLEE as a profile name.

All Tracks

Enter ROADKILL as a profile name.

All Championships

Enter REDROOSTER as a profile name.

All Challenges

Enter DOUBLEBARREL as a profile name.

Maxed Out Skill Level

Enter FIDDLERSELBOW as a profile name.

Maxed Out Stats

Enter GINGHAM as a profile name.

BALDUR'S GATE: DARK ALLIANCE

All Spells

During gameplay, hold X + Right + L all the way + R halfway.

Invincibility and Level Warp

During gameplay, hold Y + Left + L all the way + R half way, then press START.

BEACH SPIKERS

Uniforms

In World Tour, name your player one of the following to unlock bonus outfits. The name disappears when entered correctly.

Name	Uniforms
JUSTICE	105-106, Sunglasses 94

DAYTONA	107-108

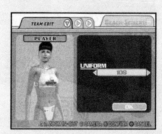

FVIPERS   109-110, Face 51, Hair 75

ARAKATA   111-113, Face 52, Hair 76

PHANTA2   114-115, Face 53, Hair 77

OHTORII   116-117

BLACK AND BRUISED

Intercontinental Mode

Select Cheat Codes from the Setup menu and press START, A (x3), Y (x3), X (x3), START.

Second Skin

Select Cheat Codes from the Setup menu and press START, A, Z, Y, X, START.

All Boxers

Select Cheat Codes from the Setup menu and press START, A, Y, X, X, Z, Z, X, Y, A, START.

Scrap Yard Scene

Select Cheat Codes from the Setup menu and press START, Y, Z, Y, Z, A, A, START.

Conversation Mode

Select Cheat Codes from the Setup menu and press START, Z, A, Y, X, Z (x3), START.

Invulnerability

Select Cheat Codes from the Setup menu and press START, A, A, Y, Y, Z, Z, X, X, START. Enter the code with Controller 2 for Invulnerability for Boxer 2.

All Boxers' Life

Select Cheat Codes from the Setup menu and press START, A, X, Y, Z, A, X, Y, Z, START.

Double Speed

Select Cheat Codes from the Setup menu and press START, Z (x10), START.

Constant Power-up

Select Cheat Codes from the Setup menu and press START, A, Y, A, Y, A, Y, X (x3), START. Enter the code with Controller 2 to get Constant Power-up for Boxer 2.

BLOODRAYNE

Cheat List

Select Cheat from the Options menu and enter the following to enable them. Pause the game to toggle the cheats.

Cheat	Enter
Gratuitous Dismemberment	INSANEGIBSMODEGOOD
Enemy Freeze	DONTFARTONOSCAR

Cheat	Enter
God Mode	TRIASSASSINDONTDIE
Juggy	JUGGYDANCESQUAD
Restore Health	LAMEYANKEEDONTFEED
Show Weapons	SHOWMEMYWEAPONS
Time Factor	NAKEDNASTYDISH
	WASHERDANCE

DEAD TO RIGHTS

From the Main menu, hold L + R and enter the following cheats:

Lazy Mode
Press Down, Left, Down, Y, Down.

10,000 Bullets Mode
Press Up, Left, Down, Right, X.

Time To Play
Press B, B, X, X, Right.

One-Shot Kill
Press Y, X, X, X, Left.

Sharpshooter Mode
Press B, B, B, Down, Right.

Bang Bang
Press X, Y, B, X, Right.

Precursor
Press Up, Up, Down, Down, Up.

Super Cop Mode
Press B, Y, Left, Up, Right.

Infinite Stamina
Press X, B, Y, X, Down.

Infinite Adrenaline
Left, Right, Left, X, B.

Bulletproof Mode

Press Up, Up, Up, B, Down.

Chow Yun Jack Mode

Press Y, X, Up, Up, Up.

Up Close and Personal Mode

Press B, Y, X, Y, B.

Extraordinary Skills

Press X, X, Up, Up, B.

Fight Club

Press Right, B, Left, X, Y.

Invisible Jack Mode

Press Y, Y, Up, Up, Y.

Boomstick Mode

Press Right, X, X, X, B.

Hard Boiled Mode

Press Y, B, Left, Left, X.

Wimp Mode

Press B, Left, Y, Up, Down.

DEF JAM VENDETTA

Arii

At the Character Select screen, hold L + R + Z and press A, Y, B, X, Y.

Carla

At the Character Select screen, hold L + R + Z and press A, Y, A (x3).

Chukklez

At the Character Select screen, hold L + R + Z and press Y, Y, B, A, X.

Cruz

At the Character Select screen, hold L + R + Z and press X, B, A, A, X.

D-Mob

At the Character Select screen, hold L + R + Z and press Y, Y, B, Y, Y.

Dan G

At the Character Select screen, hold L + R + Z and press A, X, A, X, Y.

Deebo

At the Character Select screen, hold L + R + Z and press X, X, A, A, B.

172

Deja

At the Character Select screen, hold L + R + Z and press X, Y, X, X, A.

DMX

At the Character Select screen, hold L + R + Z and press X, A, X, B, Y.

Drake

At the Character Select screen, hold L + R + Z and press A, B, B, X, X.

Funkmaster Flex

At the Character Select screen, hold L + R + Z and press X, B, X, X, Y.

Headache

At the Character Select screen, hold L + R + Z and press B (x3), Y, X.

House

At the Character Select screen, hold L + R + Z and press B, A, B, X, A.

Iceberg

At the Character Select screen, hold L + R + Z and press Y, B, X, Y, X.

Ludacris

At the Character Select screen, hold L + R + Z and press X (x3), Y, B.

Masa

At the Character Select screen, hold L + R + Z and press A, X, B, Y, Y.

Method Man

At the Character Select screen, hold L + R + Z and press Y, X, A, B, X.

Moses

At the Character Select screen, hold L + R + Z and press B, B, Y, Y, A.

N.O.R.E.

At the Character Select screen, hold L + R + Z and press X, Y, B, A, X.

Nyne

At the Character Select screen, hold L + R + Z and press Y, X, A, A, B.

Opal

At the Character Select screen, hold L + R + Z and press X, X, Y, Y, B.

Peewee

At the Character Select screen, hold L + R + Z and press A, A, Y, B, Y.

Penny

At the Character Select screen, hold L + R + Z and press A (x3), B, X.

Pockets

At the Character Select screen, hold L + R + Z and press B, Y, X, Y, A.

Razor

At the Character Select screen, hold L + R + Z and press B, Y, B, X, A.

Redman

At the Character Select screen, hold L + R + Z and press X, X, B, Y, A.

Ruffneck

At the Character Select screen, hold L + R + Z and press A, Y, A, B, X.

Scarface

At the Character Select screen, hold L + R + Z and press X, Y, A, B, Y.

Sketch

At the Character Select screen, hold L + R + Z and press B, B, X, Y, A.

Snowman

At the Character Select screen, hold L + R + Z and press B, B, A, A, X.

Steel

At the Character Select screen, hold L + R + Z and press A, B, X, X, B.

T'ai

At the Character Select screen, hold L + R + Z and press X, X, Y, A, X.

Zaheer

At the Character Select screen, hold L + R + Z and press B, B, Y, A, A.

Alternate Costume, Briggs

At the Character Select screen, hold L + R + Z and press A, B, X, Y, X.

Alternate Costume, Manny

At the Character Select screen, hold L + R + Z and press X, Y, X, Y, X.

Alternate Costume, Proof

At the Character Select screen, hold L + R + Z and press A, Y, B, Y, X.

Alternate Costume, Razor

At the Character Select screen, hold L + R + Z and press Y, X, A, B, B.

Alternate Costume, Ruffneck

At the Character Select screen, hold L + R + Z and press Y, X, B, A, Y.

Alternate Costume, Spider

At the Character Select screen, hold L + R + Z and press X, X, Y, B, B.

Alternate Costume, Tank

At the Character Select screen, hold L + R + Z and press B, Y, X, A, A.

DIE HARD: VENDETTA

Enter the following codes at the Main menu. A message appears when the code is correctly entered.

Invulnerable

At the Main menu, press L, R, L, R, L, R, L, R.

All Levels

At the Main menu, press X, Y, Z, Z, X, Y, Z, Z.

Flame On

At the Main menu, press B, X, Y, B, X, Y.

Infinite Hero Time

At the Main menu, press B, X, Y, Z, L, R.

Liquid Metal

At the Main menu, press B, Y, X, B, Y, X.

Big Heads

At the Main menu, press R, R, L, R.

Pin Heads

At the Main menu, press L, L, R, L.

Exploding Fists

At the Main menu, press R, R, Y, B, X, R, R.

Hot Fists

At the Main menu, press L, L, X, B, Y, L, L.

Kamikaze

At the Main menu, press L, R, Z, Y, B.

DR. MUTO

Select Cheats from the Options menu and enter the following:

Invincibility

Enter NECROSCI. Invincibility doesn't work when falling from high above.

Never Take Damage

Enter CHEATERBOY.

Unlock Every Gadget

Enter TINKERTOY.

Unlock Every Morph

Enter EUREKA.

Go Anywhere

Enter BEAMMEUP.

Secret Morphs

Enter LOGGLOGG.

See Movies

Enter HOTTICKET.

Super Ending

Enter BUZZOFF.

ENTER THE MATRIX

Cheat Mode

After playing through the hacking system and unlocking CHEAT.EXE, you can use CHEAT.EXE to enter the following:

Code	Enter
All Guns	0034AFFF
Infinite Ammo	1DDF2556
Invisibility	FFFFFFF1
Infinite Focus	69E5D9E4
Infinite Health	7F4DF451
Speedy Logos	7867F443
Unlock Secret Level	13D2C77F
Fast Focus Restore	FFF0020A
Test Level	13D2C77F
Enemies Can't Hear You	4516DF45
Turbo Mode	FF00001A
Multiplayer Fight	D5C55D1E
Low Gravity	BB013FFF
Taxi Driving	312MF451

EVOLUTION SKATEBOARDING

All Secret Characters

When the Konami logo appears on-screen, press Up, Up, Down, Down, Left, Right, Left, Right, B, A, B, A, Start.

GODZILLA: DESTROY ALL MONSTERS MELEE

Codes

At the Main menu, press and hold L, B, R, then release B, R, L. Enter the following codes:

Code	Enter
All Cites	480148
All Monsters (except Orga)	696924

Godzilla 2K	225133
Gigan	616233
King Ghidorah	877467
Rodan	104332
Destoroyah	537084
Mecha King Ghidorah	557456
Mecha Godzilla	131008
11 Continues	760611
Throw All Buildings & Objects	756287
P2 Invisible	459113
All Players Invisible	316022

Player Indicators Always On	135984
Indestructible Buildings	112122
Turn Military On/Off	256806
Infinite Energy for P1	677251
Infinite Energy for P2	435976
No Freeze Tanks	841720

No Display	443253
No Energy (but stronger)	650867
No Health Power-ups	562142
No Mothra Power-ups	134615
No Energy Power-ups	413403
No Rage Power-ups	119702
P1 Always Rage	649640
P2 Always Rage	122224
P3 Always Rage	548053
P4 Always Rage	451242
P1 Damage-Proof	843901
P2 Damage-Proof	706149
P3 Damage-Proof	188522
P4 Damage-Proof	286552
All Players Damage-Proof	505634
Super Energy P1	677251
Super Energy P2	435976
Super Energy P3	603696
Super Energy P4	291680
Energy	650867
P1 4X Damage	511012
P2 4x Damage	815480
P3 4x Damage	212454
P4 4x Damage	286552
All Players 4x Damage	817683
P1 Small	986875
P2 Small	971934
P3 Small	895636
P4 Small	795735
All Players Small	174204
Regenerate Health	492877
Statistics Mode	097401
Black-and-White	567980
Technicolor	661334
View Credits	176542
Game Version	097401

HULK

Cheat Codes

Select Code Input from the Options and enter the following and press Accept. Turn on the cheats by selecting Cheats from the Special Features menu.

Description	Code Input
Invulnerability	GMMSKIN
Regenerator	FLSHWND
Unlimited Continues	GRNCHTR
Double Hulk HP	HLTHDSE
Double Enemies HP	BRNGITN
Half Enemies HP	MMMYHLP
Reset High Score	NMBTHIH
Full Rage Meter	ANGMNGT
Puzzle Solved	BRCESTN
Wicked Punch	FSTOFRY
Unlock All Levels	TRUBLVR

Universal Unlock Codes

Enter the following at the special terminals, called "Universal Code Input," that are found throughout the levels. You will find these bonus materials in the Special Features menu.

Description	Code Input
Play as Gray Hulk	JANITOR
Desert Battle Art	FIFTEEN
Hulk Movie FMV Art	NANOMED
Hulk Transformed ART	SANFRAN
Hulk vs. Hulk Dogs Art	PITBULL

Note that the codes for the Hulk also work for the PlayStation 2 and Xbox versions of the game.

JAMES BOND 007: NIGHTFIRE

Select Codenames from the Main menu and pick a codename. Choose Secret Unlocks and enter the following codes. Save your codename before exiting this menu.

Level Select
Enter PASSPORT.

Alpine Escape Level
Enter POWDER.

Enemies Vanquished Level
Enter TRACTION.

Double Cross Level
Enter BONSAI.

Night Shift Level
Enter HIGHRISE.

Chain Reaction Level
Enter MELTDOWN.

Phoenix Fire Level
Enter FLAME.

Deep Descent Level
Enter AQUA.

Island Infiltration Level
Enter PARADISE.

Countdown Level
Enter BLASTOFF.

Equinox Level
Enter VACUUM.

All Gadget Upgrades
Enter Q LAB.

Camera Upgrade
Enter SHUTTER.

Decrypter Upgrade
Enter SESAME.

Grapple Upgrade
Enter LIFTOFF.

Laser Upgrade
Enter PHOTON.

Scope Upgrade
Enter SCOPE.

Stunner Upgrade
Enter ZAP.

Tranquilizer Dart Upgrade
Enter SLEEPY.

Bigger Clip for Sniper Rifle
Enter MAGAZINE.

P2K Upgrade
Enter P2000.

Golden Wolfram P2K
Enter AU P2K.

Golden PP7
Enter AU PP7.

Vanquish Car Missile Upgrade
Enter LAUNCH.

All Multiplayer Scenarios
Enter GAMEROOM.

Uplink Multiplayer Scenario

Enter TRANSMIT.

Demolition Multiplayer Scenario

Enter TNT.

Protection Multiplayer Scenario

Enter GUARDIAN.

GoldenEye Strike Multiplayer Scenario

Enter ORBIT.

Assassination Multiplayer Scenario

Enter TARGET.

Team King of the Hill Multiplayer Scenario

Enter TEAMWORK.

Explosive Scenery Option, Multiplayer

Enter BOOM. This option is in the Enviro-Mods menu.

All Characters in Multiplayer

Enter PARTY.

Play as Bond Tux, Multiplayer

Enter BLACKTIE.

Play as Drake Suit, Multiplayer

Enter NUMBER 1.

Play as Bond Spacesuit, Multiplayer

Enter ZERO G.

Play as Goldfinger, Multiplayer

Enter MIDAS.

Play as Renard, Multiplayer

Enter HEADCASE.

Play as Scaramanga, Multiplayer

Enter ASSASSIN.

Play as Christmas Jones, Multiplayer

Enter NUCLEAR.

Play as Wai Lin, Multiplayer

Enter MARTIAL.

Play as Xenia Onatopp, Multiplayer

Enter JANUS.

Play as May Day, Multiplayer

Enter BADGIRL.

Play as Elektra King, Multiplayer

Enter SLICK.

Play as Jaws, Multiplayer

Enter DENTAL.

Play as Baron Samedi, Multiplayer

Enter VOODOO.

Play as Oddjob, Multiplayer

Enter BOWLER.

Play as Nick Nack, Multiplayer

Enter BITESIZE.

Play as Max Zorin, Multiplayer

Enter BLIMP.

Drive An SUV, Enemies Vanquished Level

Start the Enemies Vanquished Level and pause the game. Hold L and press B, X, Y, B, Y, then release L.

Race in Cobra, Enemies Vanquished Level

Start the Enemies Vanquished Level and pause the game. Hold L and press X, X, B, B, Y, then release L.

Enter the following codes during the Paris Prelude, Enemies Vanquished, Island Infiltration, or Deep Descent levels:

Faster Racing

Pause the game, hold L and press B, Y, X, B, Y, X, then release L.

Berserk Racing

Pause the game, hold L and press B, Y, Y, B, Y, X, then release L.

Trails

Pause the game, hold L and press B, X, X, B, then release L.

Double Armor

Pause the game, hold L and press X, Y, B, X, X, then release L.

Triple Armor

Pause the game, hold L and press X, Y, B, X (x3), then release L.

Quadruple Armor

Pause the game, hold L and press X, Y, B, X (x4), then release L.

Super Bullets

Pause the game, hold L and press X (x4), then release L.

KELLY SLATER'S PRO SURFER

Select Cheats from the Extras screen and enter the following cell phone numbers. Turn them on and off by selecting Toggle Cheat.

Max Stats
Enter 2125551776.

High Jump
Enter 2175550217.

Perfect Balance
Enter 2135555721.

First-Person View
Enter 8775553825. Select Camera Settings from the Options screen.

Trippy
Enter 8185551447.

Mega Cheat
Enter 7145558092.

All Levels
Enter 3285554497.

All Suits
Enter 7025552918.

All Surfers
Enter 9495556799.

All Tricks
Enter 6265556043.

Surfers
Enter the following to unlock additional surfers:

Surfer	Cell Number
Freak	3105556217
Tiki God	8885554506
Tony Hawk	3235559787
Travis Pastrana	8005556292

LEGACY OF KAIN: BLOOD OMEN 2

Begin with Soul Reaver and Iron Armor

At the Main Menu press Z, R, L, B, X, Y.

LORD OF THE RINGS: THE TWO TOWERS

Health

Pause the game, hold L + R and press Y, Down, A, Up.

Arrows

Pause the game, hold L + R and press A, Down, Y, Up.

1000 Upgrade Points

Pause the game, hold L + R and press A, Down (x3).

Level 2 Skills

Pause the game, hold L + R and press X, Right, X, Right.

Level 4 Skills

Pause the game, hold L + R and press Y, Up, Y, Up.

Level 6 Skills

Pause the game, hold L + R and press B, Left, B, Left.

Level 8 Skills

Pause the game, hold L + R and press A, A, Down, Down.

To access the following codes, you must first complete the game:

Always Devastating

Pause the game, hold L + R and press B, B, X, X.

Small Enemies

Pause the game, hold L + R and press Y, Y, A, A.

All Upgrades

Pause the game, hold L + R and press Y, X, Y, X.

Invulnerable

Pause the game, hold L + R and press Y, B, A, X.

Slow Motion

Pause the game, hold L + R and press Y, X, A, B.

Unlimited Missile Weapons

Pause the game, hold L + R and press B, X, A, Y.

MAT HOFFMAN'S PRO BMX 2

Level Select

At the Title screen press B, Right, Right, Y, Down, B. This code works for Session, Free Ride, and Multiplayer modes.

Boston, MA Level (Road Trip)

At the Title screen press B, Up, Down, Down, Up, B.

Chicago, IL Level (Road Trip)

At the Title screen press B, Up, Y, Up, Y, B.

Las Vegas, NV Level (Road Trip)

At the Title screen press B, R, Left, L, Right, B.

Los Angeles, CA Level (Road Trip)

At the Title screen press B, Left, A, A, Left, B.

New Orleans, LA Level (Road Trip)

At the Title screen press B, Down, Right, Up, Left, B.

Portland, OR Level (Road Trip)

At the Title screen press Y, A, A, B, B, Y.

Day Smith

At the Title screen press Y, Up, Down, Up, Down, B.

Vanessa

At the Title screen press Y, Down, Left, Left, Down, B.

Big Foot

At the Title screen press Y, Right, Up, Right, Up, B.

The Mime

At the Title screen press Y, Left, Right, Left, Right, A.

Volcano

At the Title screen press Y, Up, Up, A, Up, Up, Y.

Street Bike

At the Title screen press A, Left, Left, L, R, Left.

Bling 540 Bike

At the Title screen press A, R, Left, Left, R, Left.

Second Costume

At the Title screen press X, L, Down, Up, R.

Elvis Costume

At the Title screen press Y, L, L, Up, Up.

BMX Costume

At the Title screen press Y, X, Left, Right, Left, X.

Tiki Battle Mode

At the Title screen press L, L, Down, Right, X, L.

Mat Hoffman Videos

At the Title screen press R, Left, Y, Left, Y, Left, R.

Joe Kowalski Videos

At the Title screen press R, Up, Y, X, Down, R.

Rick Thorne Videos

At the Title screen press R, L, R, R, L, R.

Mike Escamilla Videos

At the Title screen press R, Y, A, A, Y, A, A, R.

Simon Tabron Videos

At the Title screen press L, Z, R, L, Z, R.

Kevin Robinson Videos

At the Title screen press R, Y, X, Down, Up, R.

Cory Nastazio Videos

At the Title screen press R, X, Y, Y, X (x3), R.

Ruben Alcantara Videos

At the Title screen press R, Left, Right, Left, Right, Left, R.

Seth Kimbrough Videos

At the Title screen press R, Up, Down, Y (x3), R.

Nate Wessel Videos

At the Title screen press R, Down, B, Y, Down, B, Y, R.

All Music

At the Title screen press L, Left, Left, Right, Right, Left, A.

No Display

At the Title screen press Down, B, X, A, Y.

MEDAL OF HONOR: FRONTLINE

Select Passwords from the Options menu and enter the following. You need to turn on many of these cheats at the Bonus screen.

Silver Bullet Mode

Enter SILVERSHOT.

Bullet Shield

Enter REFLECTOR.

Mohton Torpedo

Enter BIGBOOMER.

Perfectionist

Enter FLAWLESS.

Achilles' Head

Enter HEADSUP.

Snipe-O-Rama Mode

Enter SUPERSHOT.

Rubber Grenade

Enter BOUNCE.

Men with Hats

Enter MADHATTER.

Invisible Enemies

Enter HIDENSEEK.

Mission Complete with Gold Star

Enter SEAGULL.

Mission 2: A Storm in the Port

Enter EAGLE.

Mission 3: Needle in a Haystack

Enter HAWK.

Mission 4: Several Bridges Too Far
Enter PARROT.

Mission 5: Rolling Thunder
Enter DOVE.

Mission 6: The Horten's Nest
Enter TOUCAN.

MINORITY REPORT

Select Cheats from the Special menu and enter the following:

Invincibility
Enter LRGARMS.

Level Warp All
Enter PASSKEY.

Level Skip
Enter QUITER.

All Combos
Enter NINJA.

All Weapons
Enter STRAPPED.

Infinite Ammo
Enter MRJUAREZ.

Super Damage
Enter SPINACH.

Health
Enter BUTTERUP.

Select Alternate Heroes from the Special menu to find the following codes:

Clown Hero
Enter SCARYCLOWN.

Convict Hero
Enter JAILBREAK.

GI John Hero
Enter GNRLINFANTRY.

Lizard Hero
Enter HISSSS.

Moseley Hero
Enter HAIRLOSS.

Nara Hero
Enter WEIGHTGAIN.

Nikki Hero
Enter BIGLIPS.

Robot Hero
Enter MRROBOTO.

Super John Hero
Enter SUPERJOHN.

Zombie Hero
Enter IAMSODEAD.

Free Aim
Enter FPSSTYLE.

Pain Arenas

Enter MAXIMUMHURT.

Armor

Enter STEELUP.

Baseball Bat

Enter SLUGGER.

Rag Doll

Enter CLUMSY.

Bouncy Men

Enter BOUNZMEN.

Wreck the Joint

Enter CLUTZ.

Dramatic Finish

Enter STYLIN.

Ending

Enter WIMP.

Concept Art

Enter SKETCHPAD.

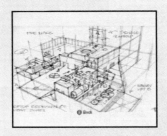

All Movies

Enter DIRECTOR.

Do Not Select

Enter DONOTSEL.

MLB SLUGFEST 20-04

Cheats

At the Match-Up screen, use B, Y and X to enter the following codes, then press the appropriate direction. For example, for "Alien Team" (231 Down) press B two times, Y three times, X one time, then press Down.

Code	Enter
Cheats Disabled	111 Down
Unlimited Turbo	444 Down
No Fatigue	343 Up
No Contact Mode	433 Left
16" Softball	242 Down

Rubber Ball	242 Up
Whiffle Bat	004 Right
Blade Bat	002 Up
Bone Bat	001 Up
Ice Bat	003 Up
Log Bat	004 Up
Mace Bat	004 Left
Spike Bat	005 Up
Big Head	200 Right
Tiny Head	200 Left
Max Batting	300 Left
Max Power	030 Left
Max Speed	003 Left
Alien Team	231 Down
Bobble Head Team	133 Down

Casey Team	233 Down
Dolphin Team	102 Down
Dwarf Team	103 Down
Eagle Team	212 Right
Evil Clown Team	211 Down
Gladiator Team	113 Down
Horse Team	211 Right

Lion Team	220 Right
Little League	101 Down
Minotaur Team	110 Down
Napalitano Team	232 Down

Olshan Team	222 Down
Pinto Team	210 Right
Rivera Team	222 Up
Rodeo Clown	132 Down
Scorpion Team	112 Down
Team Terry Fitzgerald	333 Right
Team Todd McFarlane	222 Right
Atlantis Stadium	321 Left
Coliseum Stadium	333 Up

Empire Park Stadium	321 Right
Forbidden City Stadium	333 Left
Midway Park Stadium	321 Down
Monument Stadium	333 Down
Rocket Park Stadium	321 Up
Extended Time for Codes	303 Up

NASCAR: DIRT TO DAYTONA

$10,000

At the Main menu, press Up, Down, Left, Right, Z, Left, Left.

NASCAR THUNDER 2003

Fantasy Drivers

Select Create-A-Car from the Features menu and enter EXTRA DRIVERS as a name.

Dale Earnhardt

Select Create-A-Car from the Features menu and enter DALE EARNHARDT as a name.

NBA 2K3

Codes

Select Game Play from the Options menu, hold Left on the D-pad + Right on the Left Analog Stick and press START. Exit to the Options menu and the Codes option will appear.

Sega Sports, Visual Concepts, and NBA 2K3 Teams

Enter MEGASTARS as a code.

Street Trash

Enter SPRINGER as a code.

Duotone Draw

Enter DUOTONE as a code.

NBA LIVE 2003

Create a player with the following last names. These characters will be available as free agents.

B-Rich

Enter DOLLABILLS.

Busta Rhymes

Enter FLIPMODE.

DJ Clue

Enter MIXTAPES.

Ghetto Fabulous

Enter GHETTOFAB.

Hot Karl

Enter CALIFORNIA.

Just Blaze

Enter GOODBEATS.

NBA STREET VOL. 2

Select Pick Up Game, hold L and enter the following when "Enter cheat codes now" appears at the bottom of the screen:

Unlimited Turbo

Press B, B, Y, Y.

ABA Ball

Press X, B, X, B.

WNBA Ball

Press X, Y, Y, X.

No Display Bars

Press B, X (x3).

All Jerseys
  Press X, Y, B, B.

All Courts
  Press B, Y, Y, B.

St. Lunatics Team and All Street Legends
  Press X, Y, B, Y.

All NBA Legends
  Press X, Y, Y, B.

Classic Michael Jordan
  Press X, Y, X, X.

Explosive Rims
  Press X (x3), Y.

Small Players
Press Y, Y, X, B.

Big Heads
Press X, B, B, X.

No Counters
Press Y, Y, X, X.

Ball Trails
Press Y, Y, Y, B.

All Quicks
Press Y, X, Y, B.

Easy Shots
Press Y, X, B, Y.

Hard Shots
Press Y, B, X, Y.

OUTLAW GOLF

All Characters and Clubs
Start a new game and enter Golf_Gone_Wild as a name.

Larger Ball
During gameplay, hold L and press Up (x3), Down.

Smaller Ball
During gameplay, hold L and press Down (x3), Up.

No Wind
During gameplay, hold L and press Up, Left, Down, Right, Up, Left, Down, Right, X, X.

Beating Token

During gameplay, hold L and press Z, X, Z, Z, X. This only works if you have used all of your tokens.

RED FACTION II

Select Cheats from the Extras menu and enter the following:

Unlock Everything
Enter B, B, A, A, Y, X, Y, X.

All Cheats
Enter Y, X, B, X, Y, A, B, A.

Level Select
Enter X, Y, A, B, Y, X, A, A.

Super Health
Enter A, A, Y, B, Y, B, X.

Infinite Grenades
Enter X, A, X, Y, A, X, A, X.

Director's Cut
Enter Y, A, X, B, X, A, Y, B.

Rapid Rails
Enter X, Y, X, Y, A, A, B, B.

Extra Chunky
Enter X, X, X, X, B, A, X, X.

Infinite Ammo
Enter Y, B, A, X, Y, X, A, B.

Wacky Deaths
Enter B, B, B, B, B, B, B, B.

Walking Dead
Enter A, A, A, A, A, A, A, A.

Rain Of Fire Cheat
Enter Y, Y, Y, Y, Y, Y, Y, Y.

Gibby Explosions
Enter B, X, A, Y, B, X, A, Y.

Bouncing Grenades
Enter X, X, X, X, X, X, X, X.

Gibby Ammunition
Enter A, A, A, A, X, Y, A, A.

Joker Cheat
Enter Y, A, Y, A, Y, A, Y, A.

ROBOTECH: BATTLECRY

Cheat Mode

Select New Game or Load Game, hold L + R + Z and press Left, Up, Down, A, Right, B, START. After doing so, enter the following:

Invincibility

Enter SUPERMECH.

Level Select

Enter WEWILLWIN.

All Multiplayer Levels

Enter MULTIMAYHEM.

All Models and Awards

Enter WHERESMAX.

Alternate Paint Schemes

Enter MISSMACROSS.

Gunpod Ammunition Refilled Faster

Enter SPACEFOLD.

Missiles Refilled Faster

Enter MARSBASE.

Gunpod and Missiles Refilled Faster

Enter MIRIYA.

One-Shot Kills

Enter BACKSTABBER.

One-Shot Kills, Sniper Mode

Enter SNIPER.

Upside Down

Enter FLIPSIDE.

Disable Codes

Enter CLEAR.

ROCKY

Punch Double Damage

At the Main menu, hold R and press Right, Down, Left, Up, Left, L.

Double Speed Boxing

At the Main menu, hold R and press Down, Left, Down, Up, Right, L.

All Default Boxers and Arenas

At the Main menu, hold R and press Right, Down, Up, Left, Up, L. This code *doesn't* unlock Mickey or the Rocky Statue.

All Default Boxers, Arenas, and Rocky Statue

At the Main menu, hold R and press Right (x3), Left, Right, L.

All Default Boxers, Arenas, Rocky Statue, and Mickey

At the Main menu, hold R and press Up, Down, Down, Left, Left, L.

Full Stats, Tournament and Exhibition Modes

At the Main menu, hold R and press Left, Up, Up, Down, Right, L.

Full Stats, Movie Mode

At the Main menu, hold R and press Right, Down, Down, Up, Left, L.

SCOOBY-DOO! NIGHT OF 100 FRIGHTS

All Power-ups

Pause the game, hold L + R and press X, B, X, B, X, B, B, B, X, X, B, X, X, X.

All Warp Gates

Pause the game, hold L + R and press B, B, X, B, B, X, B, X (x3).

All Movies

Pause the game, hold L + R and press B (x3), X (x3), B, X, B.

Alternate Credits

Pause the game, hold L + R and press B, X, X, B, X, B.

Holidays

Change the system date to one of the following to change the game's appearance slightly.

January 1

July 4

October 31

December 25

SONIC MEGA COLLECTION

Blue Sphere

Play Sonic 1 and Sonic 3D 20 times each.

The Comix Zone

At the Manuals screen, press Z, Z, Z, Up, Up, Up, Down, Down, Down, L, R, Z.

Flicky

Play Dr. Robotnik's Mean Bean Machine 20 times.

Ristar

Play every game 20 times.

Sonic 2 and Knuckles

Play Sonic 2 and Sonic Spinball 20 times each.

Sonic 3 and Knuckles

Play Sonic 3 and Sonic and Knuckles 20 times each.

SONIC THE HEDGEHOG

Level Select

At the Title screen, press Up, Down, Left, Right.

Debug Mode

At the Title screen, press Up, X, Down, X, Left, X, Right. Hold B, then hold START until the level loads. Press A for Debug Mode.

SONIC THE HEDGEHOG 2

Level Select

Select Sound Test from the Options menu and play the following sounds in order: 19, 65, 9, and 17. Hold X and press START. At the Title screen, hold B and press START.

Debug Mode

After enabling the Level Select code, use the Sound Test to play the following sounds in order: 1, 9, 9, 2, 1, 1, 2, 4. Select the desired level, then hold B + START until the level loads.

SONIC THE HEDGEHOG 3

Level Select

After the Sega logo fades and as Sonic appears, press Up, Up, Down, Down, Up (x4). At the Title screen, press Up to access the Level Select.

Debug Mode

With the Level Select code enabled, hold B and press Start.

SONIC SPINBALL

Level Select

At the Options menu, press B, Down, A, Down, X, Down, B, A, Up, B, X, Up, A, X, Up.

FLICKY

Level Select

Start a game and hold Up + A + X + Start. When Round I appears, release the buttons.

RISTAR

Enter the following as passwords:

Password	Code
ILOVEU	Level Select
MUSEUM	Bosses Only
SUPERB	Very Hard Difficulty
DOFEEL	Time Attack
MAGURO	Different Sounds
MIEMIE	Hidden Items
XXXXXX	Disable Codes

STAR WARS BOUNTY HUNTER

Enter the following at the Code Setup screen:

Chapter Codes

Chapter	Enter
I	SEEHOWTHEYRUN
2	CITYPLANET
3	LOCKDOWN
4	DUGSOPLENTY

| 5 | BANTHAPOODOO |
| 6 | MANDALORIANWAY |

Level Codes

Level	Enter
1	BEAST PIT
2	GIMMEMYJETPACK
3	CONVEYORAMA
4	BIGCITYNIGHTS
5	IEATNERFMEAT
6	VOTE4TRELL
7	LOCKUP
8	WHAT A RIOT
9	SHAFTED
10	BIGMOSQUITOS
11	ONEDEADDUG
12	WISHIHADMYSHIP
13	MOS GAMOS
14	TUSKENS R US
15	BIG BAD DRAGON
16	MONTROSSISBAD
17	VOSAISBADDER
18	JANGOISBADDEST

All Concept Art

Enter R ARTISTS ROCK.

All TGC Cards

Enter GO FISH.

STAR WARS: THE CLONE WARS

Select Bonuses from the Options menu, then select Codes to enter the following:

Invincibility

Enter IWITHFORCE as a password.

All Missions

Enter GASMASK as a password.

Play Ewok Freedom Song

Press Up, Up, Down, Down, Left, Right, Left, Right, B, A, START.

Team Photos

Enter SAYCHEESE.

Unlimited Ammo

Enter CHOSEN1.

All Cutscenes

Enter CINEMA.

Battle Droid in Academy

Enter ROGERROGER.

Bonus Objectives

Enter YUB YUB.

All Multiplayer Maps

Enter FRAGFIESTA.

Wookie in Academy

Enter FUZZBALL.

STAR WARS JEDI KNIGHT II: JEDI OUTCAST

Select Cheats from the Extras menu to enter the following codes:

Level Select
Enter DINGO.

Multiplayer Characters
Enter PEEPS.

Lightsaber from Beginning
Enter FUDGE.

Infinite Health
Enter BUBBLE.

Inifinite Ammo
Enter BISCUIT.

All Movies
Enter FLICKY.

First Seven Levels
Enter CHERRY.

Demo Stage
Enter DEMO.

SUPERMAN: SHADOW OF APOKOLIPS

Select Cheat Codes from the Options menu to enter the following codes:

Unlock Everything
Enter I WANT IT ALL.

All Attack Mode Stages
Enter SIGHTSEEING.

Unlimited Health
Enter FIRST AID.

Unlimited Superpower
Enter JUICED UP.

Empty Superpower
Enter JOR EL.

Disable Time Limits
Enter STOP THE CLOCK.

Slow Motion
Enter SLOW MOTION.

All Character Bios
Enter INTERVIEW.

All Movies
Enter POPCORN.

Explore Metropolis Mode
Enter WANDERER.

Shooting Gallery and Item Hunt Challenges (Explore Metropolis Mode)
Enter CREEP.

Easier Test of Strength Mode

Enter SORE FINGER.

Clark Kent

Enter SECRET IDENTITY.

Parasite

Enter FEELING DRAINED.

Extra Hard Difficulty

Enter NAILS.

Silent Movie Mode

Enter RETRO.

Reverse Controls

Enter SUPERMAN.

THE SIMPSONS: ROAD RAGE

New Year's Krusty

At the Options screen, hold L + R and press B, B, X, Y. Or, set the GameCube date to January 1.

Halloween Bart

At the Options screen, hold L + R and press B, B, X, A. Or, set the GameCube date to October 31.

Thanksgiving Marge

At the Options screen, hold L + R and press B, B, X, X. Or, set the GameCube date to Thanksgiving.

Christmas Apu

At the Options screen, hold L + R and press B, B, X, B. Or, set the GameCube date to December 25.

Flat Characters

At the Options screen, hold L + R and press X (x4).

No Map

At the Options screen, hold L + R and press Y, B, B, X.

Horizontal Split Screen, Multiplayer Mode

At the Options screen, hold L + R and press Y (x4).

Night

At the Options screen, hold L + R and press A (x4).

Alternate Camera Views

At the Options screen, hold L + R and press B (x4).

More Camera Options

At the Options screen, hold L + R and press B, A (x3).

Collision Lines

At the Options screen, hold L + R and press B, B, A, A.

Smithers in Mr. Burns's Limousine

At the Options screen, hold L + R and press B, B, Y, Y.

Nuclear Bus

At the Options screen, hold L + R and press B, B, Y, A.

Red Brick Car

At the Options screen, hold L + R and press B, B, Y, X.

Special Moves

At the Options screen, hold L1 + R1 and press A, B, B, A.

Time Trial

At the Options screen, hold L + R and press X, B, Y, A.

Slow Motion

At the Options screen, hold L + R and press A, X, B, Y.

Disable Codes

At the Options screen, hold L + R and press START (x4).

THE SIMS

At the Main Menu, press L + R to enter the following codes:

Play The Sims Mode, All 2-Player Games, Objects, and Skins

Enter MIDAS. Select Get A Life and start a new game. Join Roxy in the hot tub, pause the game and quit.

All Objects Cost Zero Simoleans

Enter FREEALL.

Party Motel, 2-Player Game

Enter PARTY M.

Play The Sims Mode
Enter SIMS.

First-Person View
Enter FISH EYE. Press X to toggle the view.

TIGER WOODS PGA TOUR 2003

Select Cheat Codes from the Options screen to enter the following:

All Golfers (Except Josey Scott) and All Courses
Enter ALLTW3.

All Golfers (Except Josey Scott)

Enter ALL28G.

All Courses

Enter 14COURSES.

Super Tiger Woods

Enter SUNDAY.

Cedric "Ace" Andrews

Enter IAM#1.

Stuart Appleby

Enter ORANGES.

Notah Begay III

Enter NOTABLY.

Mark Calavecchia

Enter CALCULATE.

Stewart Cink

Enter SINK.

Dominic "The Don" Donatello
Enter GODFATHER.

Brad Faxon
Enter XON.

Jim Furyk
Enter THESWING.

Charles Howell III
Enter BANDPANTS.

Justin Leonard
Enter JUSTINTIME.

Solita Lopez
Enter SOLITARY1.

Hamish "Mulligan" McGregor
Enter MCRUFF.

Takeharu "Tsunami" Moto
Enter 2TON.

Kellie Newman
Enter COWGIRL.

Mark O'Meara

Enter TB.

Vijay Singh

Enter VJSING.

Steve Stricker

Enter SS.

Val "Sunshine" Summers

Enter VALENTINE.

Melvin "Yosh" Tanigawa

Enter YOYOYO.

Ty Tryon

Enter TYNO.

Josey "Superstar" Scott

Enter SUPERSTAR.

TONY HAWK'S PRO SKATER 4

Select Cheat Codes from the Options screen to enter the following codes:

Unlock Everything

Enter watch_me_xplode. Find the underscore in the Symbols section.

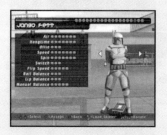

Daisy

Enter (o)(o).

Always Special

Enter GOLDEN.

Perfect Manual

Enter 2WHEELIN.

Perfect Rail

Enter BELIKEGEOFF.

Matrix Mode

Enter MRANDERSEN.

Moon Gravity

Enter GIANTSTEPS.

Secret Created Skaters

Create a new skater by entering the following names:

#$%@!	Ben Scott Pye
Aaron Skillman	Big Tex
Adam Lippmann	Brian Jennings
Andrew Skates	Captain Liberty
Andy Marchal	Chauwa Steel
Angus	Chris Peacock
Atiba Jefferson	

ConMan

Danaconda	Jason Uyeda
Dave Stohl	Jim Jagger
DDT	Joe Favazza
DeadEndRoad	John Rosser
Fritz	Jow
Gary Jesdanun	Kenzo
grjost	Kevin Mulhall
Henry Ji	Kraken
Lindsey Hayes	

Lisa G Davies	Meek West
Little Man	Mike Day
Marilena Rixfor	Mike Lashever
Mat Hoffman	Mike Ward
Matt Mcpherson	Mr. Brad
Maya's Daddy	Nolan Nelson

Parking Guy

Peasus

Pete Day

Rick Thorne

Sik

Stacey D

Zac Zig Drake

Stacey Ytuarte

Team Chicken

Ted Barber

Todd Wahoske

Top Bloke

Wardcore

TY THE TASMANIAN TIGER

Show Hidden Objects

During gameplay, press L, R, L, R, Y, Y, X, B, B, X, Z, Z.

All Abilities

During gameplay, press L, R, L, R, Y, Y, B, B, Y, B.

Technorangs

During gameplay, press L, R, L, R, Y, Y, Y, B, Y, B.

Unlimited Life

At the Main menu, press L, R, L, R, Y, Y, Y, Y, X, X.

Unlock Movies

At the Main menu, press L, R, L, R, Y, Y, A, A, Z, B, Z, B.

V-RALLY 3

Floating Cars

Enter 210741974 MARTY as a name.

Small Cars

Enter 01041977 BIGJIM as a name.

Smashed Cars

Enter 25121975 PILOU as a name.

Jelly Cars

Enter 07121974 FERGUS as a name.

Flat Cars

Enter 21051975 PTITDAV as a name.

Stretched Cars

Enter Gonzales SPEEDY as a name.

Small Cars & High-Pitched Commentary

Enter PALACH as a last name with no first name.

X2: WOLVERINE'S REVENGE

Level Select & All Challenges

At the Main menu, press B, X, B, Y, B, X, L, R, Z.

All Cerebro Files and Movies

At the Main menu, press B, X, B, Y (x3), R, R, Z.

All Costumes

At the Main menu, press B, X, B, Y (x3), L, L, Z.

Cheats

At the Main menu, press B, B, X, X, Y, Y, X, X, L, L, R, R, Z. Pause the game to find the cheats.

X-MEN: NEXT DIMENSION

Quick Death Toggle

At the Main menu, press Up, Up, Down, Down, X, Y, Y, X.

Disable AI Toggle

At the Main menu, press Up, Up, Down, Down, A, A, B, B, X, X, Y, Y.

Unlimited Supers Toggle

At the Main menu, press Up, Up, Down, Down, A, X, A, X.

Games List

Game Boy® Advance

AGGRESSIVE INLINE

All Skaters

At the Title screen, press L, L, B, B, R, R, L, R.

Level Select

At the Title screen, press Up, Down, Up, Down, Left, Right, B, R.

BALLISTIC: ECKS VS. SEVER 2

Invincibility

Enter DEATHWISH as a password.

Invisible

Enter DOYOUCME as a password.

All Weapons

Enter TOOLEDUP as a password.

Shotgun Rapid Fire

Enter MYBIGUN as a password.

Unlimited Ammunition

Enter BIGPOCKET as a password.

One-Shot Kills

Enter OOHSTOPIT as a password.

Extra Damage on Explosion

Enter ACMEBANGS as a password.

Motionless Enemies

Enter COLDFEET as a password.

Alternate Sounds

Enter HORNBLOW as a password.

Passwords

Level	Ecks	Sever
2	SMOKEY	RAVEN
3	BUTTERFLY	FIREFLY
4	COVEY	BULLDOG
5	TIGER	DRAGON
6	HORNET	LOUDMOUTH
7	LITTERBUG	STINGER
8	MUSTANG	NAIL
9	SPECTRE	ZORRO
10	NIMROD	XRAY
End	SPOOKY	REDDOG

BUBBLE BOBBLE OLD AND NEW

Bubble Bobble New: Super Mode

At the Bubble Bobble New title screen, press Right, R, Left, L, Select, R, Select, L.

Bubble Bobble Old: Original Mode

At the Bubble Bobble Old title screen, press L, R, L, R, L, R, Right, SELECT.

Bubble Bobble Old: Power-up Mode

At the Bubble Bobble Old title screen, press SELECT, R, L, Left, Right, R, SELECT, Right.

Bubble Bobble Old: Super Mode

At the Bubble Bobble Old title screen, press Left, R, Left, SELECT, Left, L, Left, SELECT.

BUTT UGLY MARTIANS: B.K.M. BATTLES

Enter the following as passwords. You can only use one password at a time.

Unlimited Lives

Enter KMIOR MAO.

Maximum Weapons, Defense, and Six Repair Kits

Enter ALWMA A15.

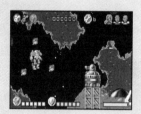

Two Extra Lives

Enter 2ELFM PLS.

Four Extra Lives

Enter IAGAW 4EL.

Two Weapon Upgrades
Enter GMACO EWU.

Four Weapon Upgrades
Enter IAGAW 4WU.

Two Defense Upgrades
Enter JT2DU 4MP.

Four Defense Upgrades
Enter DUATO U4M.

World Passwords

World	Password
2 Mechtropolis	IWTSO WN2
3 Aquatica	TMTWN 3PD
4 Arborea	IALTS MO4
5 Silicon City	IOTJO WN5
6 Magma	FILGS OW6
7 Koo Foo Ship	IWTSO WN7

CAR BATTLER JOE

Jim Joe Zero Car
In Battle League, enter TODOROKI as a password.

CASTLEVANIA:
ARIA OF SORROW

Enter the following codes as a name, then start a new game:

Use No Souls
Enter NOSOUL.

Use No Items
Enter NOUSE.

Play as Julius Belmont

After defeating the game with a good ending, enter JULIUS.

CONTRA ADVANCE

Passwords

Level	Normal Password
2	Y4HC1B L5P212 34ZWFI
3	WXJD1Z JHSJIQ KKNCYI
4	ZWJF1J MGSL1B GP3LQB
5	G3421N TDN51N C3BV2C
6	W3MJIS J4VP1N YY24BD

CT SPECIAL FORCES

Level Passwords

Level	Password
The Arid Desert	1608
The Hostile Jungle	2111
The Forbidden City	1705

Character Select Passwords

Enter the following passwords to select a character before the level.

Level	Password
Snow Covered Mountains, Level I	0202
The Hostile Jungle	2704
The Forbidden City	0108

DAVE MIRRA FREESTYLE BMX 3

Metal and Flash

At the Title screen, press R, R, L, L, B, B, L, R.

DUAL BLADES

Impossible Difficulty

At the Options screen, highlight Difficulty and press Left (x4), Right, Right, Left, Right, B.

FIRE PRO WRESTLING 2

All Wrestlers

Edit a wrestler using the following information, then save the wrestler.

Nick Name: ALL

Last Name: WRESTLER

First Name: CLEAR

Exchange: Off

Middle: NONE

FROGGER'S ADVENTURES 2: THE LOST WAND

Unlock Magician's Realm

At the Main Menu, press Up, Up, Down, Down, Left, Right, Left, Right, B, A.

GT ADVANCE 2: RALLY RACING

Extra Modes

At the Title screen, hold B + L and press Down.

All Cars

At the Title screen, hold B + L and press Left.

All Tracks

At the Title screen, hold B + L and press Right.

All Tune-Ups

At the Title screen, hold B + L and press Up.

Credits

At the Title screen, hold B + L and press Up + B.

GT ADVANCE 3: PRO CONCEPT RACING

All Cars

At the Title screen, hold L + B and press Left.

All Tracks

At the Title screen, hold L + B and press Right.

All Tune Ups

At the Title screen, hold L + B and press Up.

Extra Modes

At the Title screen, hold L + B and press Down.

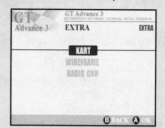

HARRY POTTER AND THE SORCERER'S STONE

10 Lives

During gameplay, press SELECT, B, A, B, A, B, B, A, A.

HE-MAN: THE POWER OF GRAYSKULL

Passwords

Level	Password
2	KMNCLDNT
3	HVDNBTTR
4	VLNTFFRT
5	FHSMBSHS
6	BHLDNGTL
7	THNKYHMN
8	THSNRSTR
9	DMGRBSGV
10	WTCHTHMN
11	FLLYRSTR
12	DMGSHRNS
13	WRKLKDMG

ICE AGE

Level Select

Enter NTTTTT as a password.

Art Gallery

Enter MFKRPH as a password.

Level Passwords

Level	Password
2	PBBQBB
3	QBCQBB
4	SBFQBB
5	DBKQBB
6	NBTQBB
7	PCTQBB
8	RFTQBB
9	CKTQBB
10	MTTQBB

IRIDION II

Easy Passwords

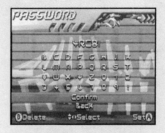

Level	Password
2	SBJS5
3	9CRT5
4	T3KG3
5	93PNV
6	95FN3
7	5MYCX
8	6C3L5
9	PW3NX
10	649QV
11	NFK2V
12	5DS2V
13	!GDV5
14	T7H8X
15	!9ROX
End	4RC8!

JUKEBOX

Enter CH4LL as a password.

JAMES BOND 007: NIGHTFIRE

Level Select

Pause the game and press R, Left, L, Right, Up, SELECT, R.

Unlimited Health

Pause the game and press R, Left, L, Right, Up, SELECT, Left.

500 Bullets

Pause the game and press R, Left, L, Right, Up, SELECT, Right.

High-Pitched Voices

Pause the game and press R, Left, L, Right, Up, SELECT, L.

JAZZ JACKRABBIT

500 Credits

Pause the game and press Right, Left, Right, Left, L, R, Up, Up, R, R, L, L.

1000 Credits

Pause the game and press Up, Down, Up, Down, Left, Right, L, R, L, R, R, L.

5000 Credits

Pause the game and press Up, Right, Down, Left, L, L, Right, Left, R, R, L, L.

JUSTICE LEAGUE: INJUSTICE FOR ALL

Invulnerability

Pause the game, highlight Resume and press SELECT, START.

MATCHBOX CROSS TOWN HEROES

Passwords

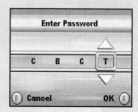

Level	Password
2	CBCT
3	QBKL
4	CBCL
5	QBVJ

6	QBDJ
End	QBVN

MEDAL OF HONOR: UNDERGROUND

Invulnerability

Enter MODEDEDIEU as a password.

Passwords

Level	Easy	Medium	Hard
1	TRILINGUE	IRRADIER	DOSSARD
2	SQUAME	FRIMAS	CUBIQUE
3	REVOLER	ESCARGOT	CHEMIN
4	FAUCON	DEVOIR	BLONDEUR
5	UNANIME	COALISER	BLESSER
6	ROULIS	BASQUE	AVOCAT
7	RELAVER	ROBUSTE	AFFINER
8	POUSSIN	SOYEUX	LAINE
9	PANOPLIE	TERRER	MESCLUN
10	NIMBER	VOULOIR	NORME
11	NIAIS	COUVERT	ORNER
12	KARMA	VOYANCE	PENNE

13	INCISER	PIGISTE	QUELQUE
14	GADOUE	NOMMER	REPOSE
15	FUSETTE	JETER	SALIFIER
16	EXCUSER	ENJAMBER	TROPIQUE
17	ENRICHIR	MORPHE	VOTATION

MIDNIGHT CLUB: STREET RACING

All Cars

Enter AGEM as a password.

NYC Passwords

Character	Password
Emilio	NIML
Larry	GTBP
Keiko	LGKG
All (opens London)	LAPC

MLB SLUGFEST 20-04

Cheats

Enter the following codes at the Matchup screen using the B, A and R buttons. For example, for All Fielders Run (132 Up), press B once, A three times and R twice, then press Up.

Effect	Code
1920 Mode	242 Up
All Fielders Run	132 Up
Backwards Fielders	444 Right
Fireworks	141 Right
Ghost Fielders	313 Down
Nuke Ball	343 Up
Skull Ball	323 Left

MORTAL KOMBAT: DEADLY ALLIANCE

25,000 Koins

Enter KWIKKASH as your name.

MUPPET PINBALL MAYHEM

Animal Machine

At the Options screen, select Credits. Then press Left, Right, Right, Up, R, Down, Down, L.

RIPPING FRIENDS

Level Select

Select Password and press Right, L, Up, Down, B, Left, Left, Right, Left.

ROBOT WARS: EXTREME DESTRUCTION

Invincibility

Create a robot with the name HARD CASE.

All Parts

Create a robot with the name SCRAP METAL.

All Arenas

Create a robot with the name GLADIATOR.

SEGA SMASH PACK

Ecco The Dolphin

Pause the game with Ecco facing the screen and press Right, B, R, B, R, Down, R, Up. This unlocks Stage Select, Sound Select, and Unlimited Lives.

Golden Axe

Select arcade mode and hold Down/Left + B and press START at the Character Select screen. This unlocks Level Select.

Golden Axe

Select arcade mode and hold Down/Left + A + R. Release the buttons and press START to gain Nine Continues.

Sonic Spinball

At the Options screen, press A, Down, B, Down, R, Down, A, B, Up, A, R, Up, B, R, Up. This unlocks Level Select. The following commands will start you at that level.

Level	Command
2 Lava Powerhouse	Hold A and press START
3 The Machine	Hold B and press START
4 Showdown	Hold R and press START

Sonic Spinball

At the Options screen, press A, Up, R, Up, L, Up, A, R, Down, A, L, Down, R, L, Down. This unlocks the game's Credits.

SPYRO: SEASON OF FLAME

Blue Spyro

At the Title screen, press Up, Up, Up, Up, Down, Left, Right, Down, B.

All Portals

At the Title screen, press Up, Left, Up, Right, Up, Down, Up, Down, B.

All Worlds in Atlas

At the Title screen, press Left, Right, Up, Up, Right, Left, Right, Up, B.

Atlas Warping

At the Title screen, press Down, Up, Left, Left, Up, Left, Left, Right, B.

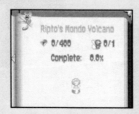

Infinite Lives

At the Title screen, press Left, Right, Left, Right (x3), Up, Down, B.

Infinite Shield for Agent 9

At the Title screen, press Left, Down, Up, Right, Left, Up, Up, Left, B.

Inifinite Ammo

At the Title screen, press Right, Left, Up, Down, Right, Down, Up, Right, B.

Never Drown

At the Title screen, press Down, Up, Right, Left, Right, Up, Right, Left, B.

All Breath Types

At the Title screen, press Right, Down, Up, Right, Left, Up, Right, Down, B.

Super Charge

At the Title screen, press Left, Left, Down, Up, Up, Right, Left, Left, B.

Dragon Draughts Mini-Game

At the Title screen, press Right, Up, Down, Down, Down, Right, Up, Down, B.

STAR WARS EPISODE 2: THE NEW DROID ARMY

After correctly entering the following passwords, you should receive an Invalid Password message.

Level Select

Enter 2D4 as a password. Use L and R to select a level.

200 Health and 200 Force

Enter 8!T as a password.

All Force Abilities

Enter FRC as a password.

Luke Skywalker

Enter SKY as a password.

Overhead Map

Enter CQL as a password.

Change Controls

Enter BTW as a password.

Disable Shadow

Enter !B4 as a password.

Black Shadows

Enter SK8 as a password.

Reduce Resolution

Enter GFX as a password.

Toggle Language Option

Enter LNG as a password. Select Language from the Options screen.

Passwords

After correctly entering the following passwords, you should receive a password accepted message.

Level	Password
Droids at Speeder	D31
Mos Espa	QK1
Xelric Draw	BKT
Womp Rat Cave	FKW
Xelric Draw	C3P
Xelric Draw	CYD
Mos Espa	AK?
Hutt's Assassins	A3W
Mos Espa	AY4
Dune Sea	KK4
Moisture Farms	M34
Moisture Farms	MYW

Jundland Wastes	TKP
Jundland Wastes	T3H
Jundland Wastes	TYQ
Jabba's Dungeon	J38
Jabba's Dungeon	JYI
Jabba's Dungeon	J?T
Jabba's Dungeon	J7J
High City	7KQ
High City	73D
High City (Interior)	7YP
High City (Interior)	7?W
Underlevels	!3C
Underlevels	!YL
Bentho's Nightclub	H3D
Core Bay	6K7
Core Bay	63L
Jedi Temple	532
Jedi Archives	4KX
Jedi Archives	438
Droid Factory Outskirts	XKI
Production Facility 1	23X
Production Facility 1	2Y7
Production Facility 2	3K2
Production Facility 2	334
Cortosis Processing Plant	WKP
Dual Duel!	W3H
Dual Duel!	WYQ
Droid Factory Core	?KH
Droid Factory Core	?3P
Duel with Vandalor	8K7
Race the Bombs	831
Ending	Y3W

SUPER PUZZLE FIGHTER 2 TURBO

The following codes work in Arcade, Vs. or Master Arcade modes.

Akuma

At the Character Select screen, press L + B.

Dan

At the Character Select screen, press L + R + B.

Devilot

At the Character Select screen, press R + B.

THE PINBALL OF THE DEAD

Boss Mode

Enter D0NTN33DM0N3Y as a password.

TOMB RAIDER: THE PROPHECY

Credits

Enter ARIA as a password.

Passwords

Level	Password
1	PRLD
2	GAZE
3	MEDI
4	HAXE
5	PATH
6	BONE
7	TREE

8	LINK
9	KURZ
10	HELL
11	WEFX
12	MEMO
13	HEAR
14	FITZ
15	ELRC
16	CLIK
17	MGSL
18	ROMA
19	MONK
20	AEON
21	TIME
22	OLIM
23	LAND
24	DART
25	HILL
26	CHEX
27	STLK
28	MECH
29	ARKD
30	MUSH
31	LITH

Looks like it is sleeping.

TREASURE PLANET

Passwords

Level	Password
1	MUSHROOM
2	TRUMPET
3	CLOUDY
4	RABBIT
5	SUNSHINE
6	SPIDER
7	APRON
8	RAINBOW
9	GOOSE
10	ENGLAND
11	MOUNTAIN
12	CAPTAIN
13	SNOWMAN
14	WITCHES
15	MONKEY
16	PRINCESS
17	WINDOW
18	COCONUT
19	FOOTBALL
20	CONCRETE
21	ELEPHANT
22	PHANTOM
23	DRAGON

URBAN YETI

Unlock Everything

Select Continue and enter TONYGOLD.

V.I.P.

Passwords

Level	Password
2	AWJW
3	Q4KT
4	PSLQ

5	TQWN
6	S3NK
7	AM3H
8	QKPI

WILD THORNBERRYS: THE MOVIE

Level Select

Enter HB5F as a password.

WOLFENSTEIN 3D

God Mode

Pause the game, hold L + R, and press A, A, B, A (x5).

All Weapons, All Keys, Full Ammo, and Full Health

Pause the game, hold L + R, and press A, B, B, A (x5).

Level Skip

Pause the game, hold L + R, and press A, B, A, A, B, B, B, A.

Skip to Boss

Pause the game, hold L + R, and press A, B, A, A, B, B, A, A.

WORMS WORLD PARTY

All Weapons

During gameplay, open the Weapon Select menu. Highlight Skip Go and press A. Return to the Weapon Select screen, hold L + Down + B, and press SELECT (x4).

X2: WOLVERINE'S REVENGE

Alternate Costumes

At the Main Menu press Up, Down, Up, Down, Left, Right, Left, Right, B, A.

YU-GI-OH! THE ETERNAL DUELIST SOUL

YU-GI-OH! WORLDWIDE EDITION: STAIRWAY TO THE DESTINED DUEL

The following passwords work for The Eternal Duelist Soul and Worldwide Edition: Stairway to the Destined Duel.

Passwords

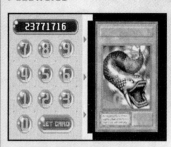 

Card	Password
7 Colored Fish	23771716
7 Completed	86198326
Acid Crawler	77568553
Acid Trap Hole	41356845
Air Eater	08353769
Air Marmot of Nefariousness	75889523
Akakieisu	38035986
Akihiron	36904469
Alligator's Sword	64428736
Alligator's Sword Dragon	03366982

Alpha The Magnet Warrior	99785935
Amazon of the Seas	17968114
Ameba	95174353
Amphibious Bugroth	40173854
Ancient Brain	42431843
Ancient Elf	93221206
Ancient Jar	81492226
Ancient Lizard Warrior	43230671
Ancient One of the Deep Forest	14015067
Ancient Telescope	17092736
Ancient Tool	49587396
Ansatsu	48365709
Anthrosaurus	89904598
Anti Raigeki	42364257
Anti-Magic Fragrance	58921041
Appropriate	48539234
Aqua Chorus	95132338
Aqua Dragon	86164529
Aqua Madoor	85639257
Arlownay	14708569
Arma Knight	36151751
Armaill	53153481
Armed Ninja	09076207
Armored Glass	36868108
Armored Lizard	15480588
Armored Rat	16246527
Armored Starfish	17535588
Armored Zombie	20277860
Axe of Despair	40619825
Axe Raider	48305365
Baby Dragon	88819587
Backup Soldier	36280194
Banisher of the Light	61528025
Barox	06840573
Barrel Dragon	81480460
Barrel Lily	67841515
Barrel Rock	10476868
Basic Insect	89091579
Battle Ox	05053103
Battle Steer	18246479
Battle Warrior	55550921
Bean Soldier	84990171
Beast Fangs	46009906
Beastking of the Swamps	99426834

Beautiful Headhuntress	16899564
Beaver Warrior	32452818
Behegon	94022093
Bell of Destruction	83555666
Beta The Magnet Warrior	39256679
Bickuribox	25655502
Big Eye	16768387
Big Insect	53606874
Big Shield Gardna	65240384
Binding Chain	08058240
Bio Plant	07670542
Black Dragon Jungle King	89832901
Black Illusion Ritual	41426869
Black Pendant	65169794
Blackland Fire Dragon	87564352
Bladefly	28470714
Blast Juggler	70138455
Blast Sphere	26302522
Block Attack	25880422
Blue Medicine	20871001
Blue-Eyed Silver Zombie	35282433
Blue-Eyes Toon Dragon	53183600
Blue-Eyes White Dragon	89631139
Blue-Eyes White Dragon	80906030
Blue-Winged Crown	41396436
Boar Soldier	21340051
Bolt Escargot	12146024
Book of Secret Arts	91595718
Bottom Dweller	81386177
Bracchio-Raidus	16507828
Breath of Light	20101223
Bright Castle	82878489
Burglar	06297941
Burning Spear	18937875
Buster Blader	78193831
Call of the Dark	78637313
Call of the Grave	16970158
Call Of The Haunted	97077563
Candle of Fate	47695416
Cannon Soldier	11384280
Castle of Dark Illusions	00062121
Castle Walls	44209392
Catapult Turtle	95727991
Ceasefire	36468556

Celtic Guardian	91152256
Ceremonial Bell	20228463
Chain Destruction	01248895
Chain Energy	79323590
Change of Heart	04031928
Charubin the Fire Knight	37421579
Chorus of Sanctuary	81380218
Claw Reacher	41218256
Clown Zombie	92667214
Cockroach Knight	33413638
Confiscation	17375316
Crass Clown	93889755
Crawling Dragon	67494157
Crawling Dragon #2	38289717
Crazy Fish	53713014
Crimson Sunbird	46696593
Crow Goblin	77998771
Crush Card	57728570
Curse of Dragon	28279543
Curse of Fiend	12470447
Curtain of the Dark Ones	22026707
Cyber Commander	06400512
Cyber Falcon	30655537
Cyber Jar	34124316
Cyber Saurus	89112729
Cyber Shield	63224564
Cyber Soldier	44865098
Cyber-Stein	69015963
Cyber-Tech Alligator	48766543
Dancing Elf	59983499
Dark Artist	72520073
Dark Assailant	41949033
Dark Chimera	32344688
Dark Elf	21417692
Dark Energy	04614116
Dark Gray	09159938
Dark Hole	53129443
D. Human	81057959
Dark King of the Abyss	53375573
Dark Magician	46986414
Dark Rabbit	99261403
Dark Sage	92377303
Dark Shade	40196604

Dark Witch	35565537
Dark Zebra	59784896
Dark-Eyes Illusionist	38247752
Darkfire Dragon	17881964
Darkfire Soldier #1	05388481
Darkfire Soldier #2	78861134
Darkness Approaches	80168720
Dark-Piercing Light	45895206
Darkworld Thorns	43500484
Deepsea Shark	28593363
Delinquent Duo	44763025
De-Spell	19159413
Destroyer Golem	73481154
Dice Armadillo	69893315
Dimensional Warrior	37043180
Disk Magician	76446915
Dissolverock	40826495
DNA Surgery	74701381
Dokuroizo the Grim Reaper	25882881
Doma The Angel of Silence	16972957
Doron	00756652
Dorover	24194033
Dragon Capture Jar	50045299
Dragon Piper	55763552
Dragon Seeker	28563545
Dragon Treasure	01435851
Dragon Zombie	66672569
Dragoness the Wicked Knight	70681994
Dream Clown	13215230
Driving Snow	00473469
Drooling Lizard	16353197
Dryad	84916669
Dunames Dark Witch	12493482
Dungeon Worm	51228280
Dust Tornado	60082869
Earthshaker	60866277
Eatgaboon	42578427
Eldeen	06367785
Electric Lizard	55875323
Electric Snake	11324436
Electro-Whip	37820550
Elegant Egotist	90219263
Elf's Light	39897277
Empress Judge	15237615

Enchanted Javelin	96355986
Enchanting Mermaid	75376965
Eradicating Aerosol	94716515
Eternal Draught	56606928
Eternal Rest	95051344
Exchange	05556668
Exile of the Wicked	26725158
Exodia the Forbidden One	33396948
Eyearmor	64511793
Fairy Dragon	20315854
Fairy's Hand Mirror	17653779
Fairywitch	37160778
Faith Bird	75582395
Fake Trap	03027001
Feral Imp	41392891
Fiend Kraken	77456781
Fiend Reflection #1	68870276
Fiend Reflection #2	02863439
Fiend Sword	22855882
Fiend's Hand	52800428
Final Flame	73134081
Fire Kraken	46534755
Fire Reaper	53581214
Firegrass	53293545
Fireyarou	71407486
Fissure	66788016
Flame Cerebrus	60862676
Flame Champion	42599677
Flame Ghost	58528964
Flame Manipulator	34460851
Flame Swordsman	45231177
Flame Viper	02830619
Flash Assailant	96890582
Flower Wolf	95952802
Flying Kamakiri #1	84834865
Flying Kamakiri #2	03134241
Follow Wind	98252586
Forced Requisition	74923978
Forest	87430998
Frenzied Panda	98818516
Fusion Sage	26902560
Fusionist	01641882
Gaia Power	56594520
Gaia the Dragon Champion	66889139

Gaia the Fierce Knight	06368038
Gale Dogra	16229315
Gamma the Magnet Warrior	11549357
Ganigumo	34536276
Garma Sword	90844184
Garma Sword Oath	78577570
Garnecia Elefantis	49888191
Garoozis	14977074
Garvas	69780745
Gatekeeper	19737320
Gazelle the King of Mythical Beasts	05818798
Gemini Elf	69140098
Genin	49370026
Germ Infection	24668830
Ghoul with an Appetite	95265975
Giant Flea	41762634
Giant Germ	95178994
Giant Mech-Soldier	72299832
Giant Rat	97017120
Giant Red Seasnake	58831685
Giant Scorpion of the Tundra	41403766
Giant Soldier of Stone	13039848
Giant Trunade	42703248
Giant Turtle Who Feeds on Flames	96981563
Gift of The Mystical Elf	98299011
Giganto	33621868
Giga-tech Wolf	08471389
Giltia the D. Knight	51828629
Goblin Fan	04149689
Goblin's Secret Remedy	11868825
Goddess of Whim	67959180
Goddess with the Third Eye	53493204
Gokibore	15367030
Graceful Charity	79571449
Graceful Dice	74137509
Grappler	02906250
Gravedigger Ghoul	82542267
Gravekeeper's Servant	16762927
Graverobber	61705417
Graveyard and the Hand of Invitation	27094595
Great Bill	55691901
Great Mammoth of Goldfine	54622031
Great White	13429800
Green Phantom King	22910685

Greenkappa	61831093
Griffore	53829412
Griggle	95744531
Ground Attacker Bugroth	58314394
Gruesome Goo	65623423
Gryphon Wing	55608151
Guardian of the Labyrinth	89272878
Guardian of the Sea	85448931
Guardian of the Throne Room	47879985
Gust	73079365
Gust Fan	55321970
Gyakutenno Megami	31122090
Hane-Hane	07089711
Haniwa	84285623
Happy Lover	99030164
Hard Armor	20060230
Harpie Lady	76812113
Harpie Lady Sisters	12206212
Harpie's Brother	30532390
Harpie's Feather Duster	18144506
Harpie's Pet Dragon	52040216
Heavy Storm	19613556
Hercules Beetle	52584282
Hero of the East	89987208
Hibikime	64501875
High Tide Gyojin	54579801
Hinotama	46130346
Hinotama Soul	96851799
Hiro's Shadow Scout	81863068
Hitodenchak	46718686
Hitotsu-Me Giant	76184692
Holograh	10859908
Horn Imp	69669405
Horn of Heaven	98069388
Horn of Light	38552107
Horn of the Unicorn	64047146
Hoshiningen	67629977
Hourglass of Courage	43530283
Hourglass of Life	08783685
House of Adhesive Tape	15083728
Hunter Spider	80141480
Hyo	38982356
Hyosube	02118022
Hyozanryu	62397231

Ice Water	20848593
Ill Witch	81686058
Illusionist Faceless Mage	28546905
Imperial Order	61740673
Insect Armor with Laser Cannon	03492538
Insect Queen	91512835
Insect Soldiers of the Sky	07019529
Inspection	16227556
Invader from Another Dimension	28450915
Invader of the Throne	03056267
Invigoration	98374133
Jellyfish	14851496
Jigen Bakudan	90020065
Jinzo	77585513
Jinzo #7	32809211
Jirai Gumo	94773007
Judge Man	30113682
Just Desserts	24068492
Kagemusha of the Blue Flame	15401633
Kageningen	80600490
Kairyu-Shin	76634149
Kaiser Dragon	94566432
Kamakiriman	68928540
Kaminari Attack	09653271
Kaminarikozou	15510988
Kamionwizard	41544074
Kanikabuto	84103702
Karate Man	23289281
Karbonala Warrior	54541900
Kattapillar	81179446
Key Mace #2	20541432
Killer Needle	88977991
King Fog	84686841
King of Yamimakai	69455834
Kiseitai	04266839
Kojikocy	01184620
Kotodama	19406822
Koumori Dragon	67724379
Krokodilus	76512652
Kumootoko	56283725
Kunai with Chain	37390589
Kurama	85705804
Kuriboh	40640057
Kwagar Hercules	95144193

La Jinn the Mystical Genie of the Lamp	97590747
Labyrinth Tank	99551425
Lady of Faith	17358176
LaLa Li-oon	09430387
Larvae	94675535
Laser Cannon Armor	77007920
Last Day of Witch	90330453
Last Will	85602018
Laughing Flower	42591472
Launcher Spider	87322377
Lava Battleguard	20394040
Left Arm of the Forbidden One	07902349
Left Leg of the Forbidden One	44519536
Legendary Sword	61854111
Leghul	12472242
Leogun	10538007
Lesser Dragon	55444629
Light of Intervention	62867251
Lightforce Sword	49587034
Liquid Beast	93108297
Little Chimera	68658728
Little D	42625254
Lord of D	17985575
Lord of the Lamp	99510761
Lord of Zemia	81618817
Luminous Spark	81777047
Lunar Queen Elzaim	62210247
Mabarrel	98795934
Machine Conversion Factory	25769732
Machine King	46700124
Magic Jammer	77414722
Magic Thorn	53119267
Magical Ghost	46474915
Magical Hats	81210420
Magical Labyrinth	64389297
Magic-Arm Shield	96008713
Magician of Faith	31560081
Maha Vailo	93013676
Maiden of the Moonlight	79629370
Major Riot	09074847
Malevolent Nuzzler	99597615
Mammoth Graveyard	40374923
Man Eater	93553943

Man-Eater Bug	54652250
Man-Eating Black Shark	80727036
Man-Eating Plant	49127943
Man-Eating Treasure Chest	13723605
Manga Ryu-Ran	38369349
Marine Beast	29929832
Masaki the Legendary Swordsman	44287299
Mask of Darkness	28933734
Masked Sorcerer	10189126
Master & Expert	75499502
Mavelus	59036972
Mechanical Snail	34442949
Mechanical Spider	45688586
Mechanicalchaser	07359741
Meda Bat	76211194
Mega Thunderball	21817254
Megamorph	22046459
Megazowler	75390004
Meotoko	53832650
Mesmeric Control	48642904
Messenger of Peace	44656491
Metal Detector	75646520
Metal Dragon	09293977
Metal Fish	55998462
Metal Guardian	68339286
Metalmorph	68540058
Metalzoa	50705071
Millennium Golem	47986555
Millennium Shield	32012841
Milus Radiant	07489323
Minar	32539892
Minomushi Warrior	46864967
Mirror Force	44095762
Mirror Wall	22359980
Misairuzame	33178416
Molten Destruction	19384334
Monster Egg	36121917
Monster Eye	84133008
Monster Reborn	83764718
Monster Tamer	97612389
Monstrous Bird	35712107
Moon Envoy	45909477
Mooyan Curry	58074572
Morinphen	55784832

Morphing Jar	33508719
Morphing Jar #2	79106360
Mother Grizzly	57839750
Mountain	50913601
Mountain Warrior	04931562
Mr. Volcano	31477025
Muka Muka	46657337
Mushroom Man	14181608
Mushroom Man #2	93900406
Musician King	56907389
M-Warrior #1	56342351
M-Warrior #2	92731455
Mysterious Puppeteer	54098121
Mystic Horseman	68516705
Mystic Lamp	98049915
Mystic Plasma Zone	18161786
Mystic Probe	49251811
Mystic Tomato	83011277
Mystical Capture Chain	63515678
Mystical Elf	15025844
Mystical Moon	36607978
Mystical Sand	32751480
Mystical Sheep #1	30451366
Mystical Sheep #2	83464209
Mystical Space Typhoon	05318639
Needle Ball	94230224
Needle Worm	81843628
Negate Attack	14315573
Nekogal #1	01761063
Nekogal #2	43352213
Nemuriko	90963488
Neo the Magic Swordsman	50930991
Nimble Momonga	22567609
Niwatori	07805359
Nobleman of Crossout	71044499
Nobleman of Extermination	17449108
Numinous Healer	02130625
Octoberser	74637266
Ocubeam	86088138
Ogre of the Black Shadow	45121025
One-Eyed Shield Dragon	33064647
Ooguchi	58861941
Ookazi	19523799
Orion the Battle King	02971090

Oscillo Hero	82065276
Oscillo Hero #2	27324313
Painful Choice	74191942
Pale Beast	21263083
Panther Warrior	42035044
Paralyzing Potion	50152549
Parasite Paracide	27911549
Parrot Dragon	62762898
Patrol Robo	76775123
Peacock	20624263
Pendulum Machine	24433920
Penguin Knight	36039163
Penguin Soldier	93920745
Petit Angel	38142739
Petit Dragon	75356564
Petit Moth	58192742
Polymerization	24094653
Pot of Greed	55144522
Power of Kaishin	77027445
Pragtical	33691040
Premature Burial	70828912
Prevent Rat	00549481
Princess of Tsurugi	51371017
Prisman	80234301
Prohibition	43711255
Protector of the Throne	10071456
Psychic Kappa	07892180
Pumpking the King of Ghosts	29155212
Punished Eagle	74703140
Queen Bird	73081602
Queen of Autumn Leaves	04179849
Queen's Double	05901497
Raigeki	12580477
Raimei	56260110
Rainbow Flower	21347810
Raise Body Heat	51267887
Rare Fish	80516007
Ray & Temperature	85309439
Reaper of the Cards	33066139
Red Archery Girl	65570596
Red Medicine	38199696
Red-Eyes Black Dragon	74677422
Red-Eyes Black Metal Dragon	64335804
Reinforcements	17814387

Relinquished	64631466
Remove Trap	51482758
Respect Play	08951260
Restructer Revolution	99518961
Reverse Trap	77622396
Rhaimundos of the Red Sword	62403074
Right Arm of the Forbidden One	70903634
Right Leg of the Forbidden One	08124921
Ring of Magnetism	20436034
Riryoku	34016756
Rising Air Current	45778932
Roaring Ocean Snake	19066538
Robbin' Goblin	88279736
Rock Ogre Grotto #1	68846917
Rogue Doll	91939608
Root Water	39004808
Rose Spectre of Dunn	32485271
Royal Decree	51452091
Royal Guard	39239728
Rude Kaiser	26378150
Rush Recklessly	70046172
Ryu-Kishin	15303296
Ryu-Kishin Powered	24611934
Ryu-Ran	02964201
Saber Slasher	73911410
Saggi the Dark Clown	66602787
Salamandra	32268901
Sand Stone	73051941
Sangan	26202165
Sea Kamen	71746462
Sea King Dragon	23659124
Seal of the Ancients	97809599
Sebek's Blessing	22537443
Sectarian of Secrets	15507080
Senju of the Thousand Hands	23401839
Seven Tools of the Bandit	03819470
Shadow Specter	40575313
Share the Pain	56830749
Shield & Sword	52097679
Shining Fairy	95956346
Shovel Crusher	71950093
Silver Bow and Arrow	01557499
Silver Fang	90357090
Sinister Serpent	08131171

Skelengel	60694662
Skelgon	32355828
Skull Dice	00126218
Skull Red Bird	10202894
Skull Servant	32274490
Skull Stalker	54844990
Skullbird	08327462
Sleeping Lion	40200834
Slot Machine	03797883
Snake Fang	00596051
Snakeyashi	29802344
Snatch Steal	45986603
Sogen	86318356
Solemn Judgment	41420027
Solitude	84794011
Solomon's Lawbook	23471572
Sonic Bird	57617178
Sonic Maid	38942059
Soul Hunter	72869010
Soul of the Pure	47852924
Soul Release	05758500
Sparks	76103675
Spear Cretin	58551308
Spellbinding Circle	18807108
Spike Seadra	85326399
Spirit of the Books	14037717
Spirit of the Harp	80770678
Stain Storm	21323861
Star Boy	08201910
Steel Ogre Grotto #1	29172562
Steel Ogre Grotto #2	90908427
Steel Scorpion	13599884
Steel Shell	02370081
Stim-Pack	83225447
Stone Armadiller	63432835
Stone Ogre Grotto	15023985
Stop Defense	63102017
Stuffed Animal	71068263
Succubus Knight	55291359
Summoned Skull	70781052
Supporter in the Shadows	41422426
Swamp Battleguard	40453765
Sword Arm of Dragon	13069066
Sword of Dark Destruction	37120512

Sword of Deep-Seated	98495314
Sword of Dragon's Soul	61405855
Swords of Revealing Light	72302403
Swordsman from a Foreign Land	85255550
Swordstalker	50005633
Tailor of the Fickle	43641473
Tainted Wisdom	28725004
Takriminos	44073668
Takuhee	03170832
Tao the Chanter	46247516
Temple of Skulls	00732302
Tenderness	57935140
Terra the Terrible	63308047
The 13th Grave	00032864
The Bewitching Phantom Thief	24348204
The Bistro Butcher	71107816
The Cheerful Coffin	41142615
The Drdek	08944575
The Eye of Truth	34694160
The Flute of Summoning Dragon	43973174
The Forceful Sentry	42829885
The Furious Sea King	18710707
The Immortal of Thunder	84926738
The Inexperienced Spy	81820689
The Little Swordsman of Aile	25109950
The Regulation of Tribe	00296499
The Reliable Guardian	16430187
The Shallow Grave	43434803
The Snake Hair	29491031
The Stern Mystic	87557188
The Thing That Hides in the Mud	18180762
The Unhappy Maiden	51275027
The Wandering Doomed	93788854
The Wicked Worm Beast	06285791
Three-Headed Geedo	78423643
Three-Legged Zombies	33734439
Thunder Dragon	31786629
Tiger Axe	49791927
Time Machine	80987696
Time Seal	35316708
Time Wizard	71625222
Toad Master	62671448
Togex	33878931

Toll	82003859
Tomozaurus	46457856
Tongyo	69572024
Toon Alligator	59383041
Toon Mermaid	65458948
Toon Summoned Skull	91842653
Toon World	15259703
Torike	80813021
Total Defense Shogun	75372290
Trakadon	42348802
Trap Hole	04206964
Trap Master	46461247
Trent	78780140
Trial of Nightmare	77827521
Tribute to the Doomed	79759861
Tripwire Beast	45042329
Turtle Tiger	37313348
Twin Long Rods #2	29692206
Twin-Headed Fire Dragon	78984772
Twin-Headed Thunder Dragon	54752875
Two-Headed King Rex	94119974
Two-Mouth Darkruler	57305373
Two-Pronged Attack	83887306
Tyhone	72842870
Tyhone #2	56789759
UFO Turtle	60806437
Ultimate Offering	80604091
Umi	22702055
Umiiruka	82999629
Unknown Warrior of Fiend	97360116
Upstart Goblin	70368879
Uraby	01784619
Ushi Oni	48649353
Valkyrion the Magna Warrior	75347539
Vermillion Sparrow	35752363
Versago the Destroyer	50259460
Vile Germs	39774685
Violent Rain	94042337
Violet Crystal	15052462
Vishwar Randi	78556320
Vorse Raider	14898066
Waboku	12607053
Wall of Illusion	13945283

Warrior Elimination	90873992
Warrior of Tradition	56413937
Wasteland	23424603
Water Element	03732747
Water Girl	55014050
Water Magician	93343894
Water Omotics	02483611
Waterdragon Fairy	66836598
Weather Control	37243151
Weather Report	72053645
Whiptail Crow	91996584
White Hole	43487744
White Magical Hat	15150365
Wicked Mirror	15150371
Widespread Ruin	77754944
Windstorm of Etaqua	59744639
Wing Egg Elf	98582704
Winged Cleaver	39175982
Winged Dragon, Guardian of the Fortress #1	87796900
Wings of Wicked Flame	92944626
Witch of the Black Forest	78010363
Witch's Apprentice	80741828
Witty Phantom	36304921
Wodan the Resident of the Forest	42883273
Wood Remains	17733394
World Suppression	12253117
Wow Warrior	69750536
Wretched Ghost of the Attic	17238333
Yado Karu	29380133
Yaiba Robo	10315429
Yamatano Dragon Scroll	76704943
Yami	59197169
Yaranzo	71280811
Zanki	30090452
Zoa	24311372
Zombie Warrior	31339260
Zone Eater	86100785

An Imprint of Pearson Education
201 West 103rd Street
Indianapolis, Indiana 46290

PlayStation® and PlayStation® 2 are registered trademarks of Sony Computer Entertainment Inc. Xbox™ is a trademark of Microsoft Corporation. Nintendo GameCube™ and GameBoy® Advance are trademarks or registered trademarks of Nintendo of America Inc.

All products, characters, and game titles mentioned in this book are trademarks of their respective companies.

Please be advised that the ESRB rating icons, "E", "K-A", "T", "M", and "AO" are copyrighted works and certification marks owned by the Interactive Digital Software Association and the Entertainment Software Rating Board and may only be used with their permission and authority. Under no circumstances may the rating icons be self-applied to any product that has not been rated by the ESRB. For information regarding whether a product has been rated by the ESRB, please call the ESRB at (212) 759-0700 or 1-800-771-3772. Please note that ESRB ratings only apply to the content of the game itself and do NOT apply to the content of the books.

ISBN: 0-7440-0269-9

Library of Congress Catalog No.: 2002113430

Printing Code: The rightmost double-digit number is the year of the book's printing; the rightmost single-digit number is the number of the book's printing. For example, 03-1 shows that the first printing of the book occurred in 2003.

06 05 04 03   4 3 2 1

Manufactured in the United States of America.

BradyGAMES Staff

Publisher
David Waybright

Editor-In-Chief
H. Leigh Davis

Creative Director
Robin Lasek

Marketing Manager
Janet Eshenour

Licensing Manager
Mike Degler

Assistant Marketing Manager
Susie Nieman

Credits

Title Manager
Tim Cox

Screenshot Editor
Michael Owen

Book Designer
Carole Stamile

Production Designers
Amy Hassos
Tracy Wehmeyer